LOST SON?

A Bastard Child's Journey of *Hope, Search, Discovery, and Healing*

By
Lawrence P. Adams

PublishAmerica
Baltimore

First printing

ISBN: 1-4137-1709-8
PUBLISHED BY PUBLISHAMERICA, LLLP
www.publishamerica.com
Baltimore

Printed in the United States of America

This book is dedicated to:

The memory of my maternal birth family
I was never privileged to know.

Ms. Genevieve Condon, Mr. Clarence Weinerth, and Msgr.
Nicholas H. Wegner, Boys Town teachers,
and the late former Executive Director of Boys Town
who took it upon themselves to take a young man under siege
in his life and teach him to reach for his fullest potential.

Mrs. Ann Piechowiak, the first person
who nudged and prodded the author to tell his story.

My cousin Carol Goulet, who spent untold hours
editing this book!

To Paulie
a Sweetheart
always reach for
your dreams!
Peace
Lawrence P. [illegible]
6/05/04

Table of Contents

Chapter One

EARLY YEARS

We all have a family tree. Just as the fruit on a tree falls to the ground, we too sometimes lose our connections. However, the tree and roots are still there. This is the story of the *Lost Son*.

Newark International Airport...the day has arrived...36 years, 3 months, and 17 days after I was born...I would meet the woman who gave me life. To say I was tense or nervous would be putting it mildly. I arrived at the airport hours before the flight was due to arrive. I brought with me 36 long-stemmed red roses, one for each year of life I had been blessed with. Should I call her Mother? Should I hug her? What should I do?

This is not the end of the story; it is only the end of one journey within the story. In order to get the full meaning of this day one needs to go back 36 years, 3 months, and 17 days, the day I was born, which began a childhood of no family to ever call my own...finding out I belonged to no one!

I was born on February 7, 1950, in Detroit, Michigan. I was born to a mother and father whom I would not know until the scene described above. I was born to an unwed mother at Providence Hospital. I was given the name of Lawrence Philip Adams. My mother was all of nineteen years old. My birth would not be greeted with great joy as so many births are. My mother had no place she could call home to take me. She had no way to support herself, yet alone a newborn. She had earlier faced the difficult decision of whether to carry a child to birth or to abort. Now she faced the gut-wrenching decision to give her newborn son up for adoption. After a process only a mother can fully appreciate, she gave me up only moments after my birth.

I would remain in the nursery of Providence Hospital for the first six months of my life. Though my mother had given me up for adoption, there was no family ready to adopt me. On June 7, 1950, four months after birth, a petition was made to the court alleging that "the child's mother is unmarried and without adequate provision for care and support." I was placed in custody of the court. In August of 1950 I would be transferred to the nursery of the Sarah Fisher Home in Farmington, Michigan. This was where my mother had spent her last months of pregnancy since at that time it was officially known as a home for unwed mothers.

I would spend these first months of life without bonding to a mother but in the care of others. Yes, they provided for my basic needs, though I doubt they provided what I needed most at that time: love!

Finally, just a few weeks shy of my first birthday I was moved from institutional care to that of my first foster parents. By the time my second birthday would roll around I had been transferred three more times to different foster parents. On August 1, 1952, I was placed in the home of what was finally to be my adoptive parents. For reasons not made available to me, four months later I was returned as a ward of the court and returned to the foster parents who cared for me just prior to my supposed adoption.

Over the next four years I would be transferred four more times to different foster parents, only to end up once again being returned to foster parents who had cared for me twice before. I would remain with these foster parents for the next four years...until age ten.

The fourteen moves, in eleven years, are listed below:

2/7/50 - 8/10/50: Providence Hospital Nursery
8/10/50 - 1/19/51: Sarah Fisher Home Nursery
1/19/51 - 7/11/51: Foster Home #1: Turner Home

7/11/51 - 9/10/51: Foster Home #2: McVicor Home
9/10/51 - 2/20/52: Foster Home #3: Kennedy Home
2/20/52 - 8/1/52: Foster Home #4: Monshor Home
8/1/52 - 12/11/52: Foster/Adoptive Home #5: Bellmeyer Home
12/11/52 - 11/26/54: Foster Home #6: Monshor Home
11/26/54 - 1/26/55: Foster Home #7: Keegan Home
1/26/55 - 8/12/55: Foster Home #8: Wagner Home
8/12/55 - 5/4/56: Foster Home #9: Adelman Home
5/4/56 - 5/17/60: Foster Home #10: Monshor Home
5/17/60 - 7/22/60: Juvenile Detention Center awaiting new foster home
7/22/60 - 4/16/61: Foster Home #11: McCann Home
4/16/61 - 6/4/68: Boys Town, Nebraska
6/4/68: Adult; released as a ward of Catholic Social Services of Wayne County, Michigan…FREE AT LAST!

It was also at this time that I came to recognize that I was a "bag boy." This is the term still used by foster children today. When one goes to a foster home you always leave your bag packed, knowing you could be unexpectedly removed from the home. Back in the 1950s it was a paper grocery bag you kept packed. All your worldly possessions could usually fit in one, as you didn't have much to call your own in the first place. When a social worker came to the home to get you they always said, "Go get your bag." No wonder I don't want anything I buy today in a paper bag…paper bags still bring up sad memories. Foster parents were allowed to take a foster child twice a year to St. Vincent de Paul Society to obtain clothing at no expense to them. They were allowed to pick out 2 dress pants, 1 pair of jeans, 3 sets of underwear and socks, 3 shirts for school and 2 t-shirts for play each time they came. One time a year they could get 1 pair of school shoes and 1 winter jacket. These were what were kept in our "bag" at each home we went. They also provide freebies such as toothbrushes, toothpaste and combs. Sometimes, if you were lucky, a foster parent would purchase you clothes out of their own money. I usually had space to spare in "my bag."

From 1956-1960 my life had a degree of stability, though I could be snapped up and removed to another home at any time. It was during these years I remember thinking for the first time, "Why was I not a member of any one family?" "Why didn't anyone want me?" "Why didn't anyone love me enough to call me their son?"

Other than my memories of the years spent with the Monshors and Foster Home #11, I have no memory of any of the other foster homes. I know they provided at least the basics of life for me or I might not be here. I don't know how caring or loving they might have been. I doubt much just from the shortness of time I spent with most. I am grateful to them, however, for without them providing at least a temporary home for me, even for a short period of time, who knows where I might be today.

Chapter Two

MOM and DAD MONSHOR

This chapter is dedicated to Mom and Dad Monshor, who provided me the only positive, loving experience of my childhood. Although they were not allowed to adopt me legally, they did so within their hearts, as I adopted them within mine. From the day of my birth until shortly past my eleventh birthday, I was moved to eleven foster homes and four institutions. One of the foster homes I was fortunate to be moved to three times and spend a total of 6½ years at, was the home of Mom and Dad Monshor.

I began this chapter calling Ernest and Mildred Monshor Mom and Dad. They will always be Mom and Dad to me. Although they were never allowed to adopt me and I was removed from their home three times, they are the only people I have ever considered my parents. I loved them as a child, I love them even more now as an adult and I will love them until I take my final breath.

I first came to their home days after my second birthday, remaining there six months before being moved.

After four brief months with tentative adoptive parents, I was returned to their home where I would remain for two years. I was removed a second time in 1954 and moved to three different foster homes in the next 1½ years. In 1956, I was returned to the Monshor home and would remain there for the next four years.

My second and third times with the Monshor family were the most stable times in my short life to that point.

They were also the most loving times. I know I was not considered just another foster child. I was treated and loved as one of their own. At the time Mom and Dad had a grown son (Sonny), an adopted son (Dennis) and two adopted daughters (Susan and Genevieve).

Over the years, they had also taken in over thirty foster children for various lengths of time. No matter how long you were with them, you were considered and treated as a member of their family. There are many fond memories of my childhood years with Mom and Dad.

As a small tike, I was sickly, having whooping cough more than once. The doctors feared I might die from it. There were many nights when the coughing would begin; Mom would get up from her bed to carry me in her arms over her shoulder, gently patting my back until the coughing stopped. This could occur more than once a night.

It was Mom and Dad who recognized I had a problem with my left eye (lazy eye) and saw to it that steps were taken to try and correct it. I underwent five surgeries and therapy. Unfortunately it was to no avail.

Mom sat with me the night before I was to have my tonsils removed, comforting me as I was a scared five-year-old, and seeing to it that there was ice cream and a smile for me when I came out of surgery.

On Sundays, the kids would all be sent to church. When we came home, we went to the downstairs kitchen to gather around the large rectangular table. We watched while Dad stirred his infamous big pot of spaghetti sauce, ready to feed the troops. It was so, so good! Dad was a cook in the US Army during World War II and was excellent.

Their adopted son Dennis died in 1954 at age 14 due to an enlarged heart. Though I have no recollections, Mom and Dad told me later of the closeness Dennis and I had, and how protective he always was of me.

I was confirmed in the Catholic church early in 1960 by Cardinal Deardon of Detroit. I did not tell anyone prior to the ceremony the name I had chosen to take for my confirmation name. Afterwards I told Mom and Dad I took the name Dennis to remember him and to honor them. I still remember Dad's broad smile and Mom being Mom, all teary eyed.

Their son Raymond proposed to Marge at Christmas 1953. I didn't understand what he was doing, so I asked. When I found out, I remember telling him, "No, you can't have her...she's my gal!" I loved his fiancé and whenever she came over, I ran to her and clung to her. She was very special.

During the last four years of a somewhat stable home environment, I started school. I attended kindergarten through third grade at St. Gabriel. Mom would sit with us kids after dinner around the table and help us complete our homework assignments, baths, bedtime prayers and bed soon followed.

Many nights, Mom would come to my bed to tuck me in and to sing me to sleep. Her favorite was a revised song containing the words of "When I was just a little boy, I asked my mother, what would I be, here's what she said to me." I still find myself humming that song today when I am feeling really down in the dumps...it usually brings me out of it and puts a smile on my face.

Then there were trips in Dad's 1957 Studebaker. It was black and hot in the summer. It was before the days of air-conditioned cars. How I enjoyed those rides with hot air blowing in my face...NOT!

Mom so tenderly planted and cared for her garden. Each spring the backyard would come alive with color.

I was removed from Mom and Dad's home a second time a month before Christmas in 1954. I have no memory of Christmas 1954 or 1955.

I do remember Christmas 1956, however, as I was back home. The Saturday before Christmas, Susan, Genevieve and I were sent over to St. Gabriel School for a Christmas program. When we left the house, it was devoid of anything Christmas. What a difference when we returned a few short hours later.

Outside Dad had strung Christmas lights...the big old-fashioned ones. Inside, the tree had been decked in its Christmas finest. On the fireplace were hung five stockings. Inscribed on each was: Mom, Dad, Daughter, Daughter and Son.

I remember asking Mom, "Who is the son stocking for, Sonny?"

Mom said, "No, that is for YOU!"

My heart still feels the love and warmth of that statement. I don't remember what I got that Christmas, but the most important thing I received was *love*. I have no childhood memories of other Christmases…this one was/is special.

In the early fall of the year Mom pulled out the canning jars, then spent hours cooking and canning beans, tomatoes, beets and peaches, to name a few. She also made batches of applesauce and an out-of-this-world apple butter.

At the same time, Dad would be making his chili sauce of tomatoes, onions, red/green papers…like today's salsa. Dad was making it long before it became popular.

I can still almost smell the alluring aroma of Mom's apple pies. They were both great cooks.

Back then, parents were parents. In the pantry, on a hook, was Dad's old Army strap. Neither Mom nor Dad were bashful in using it if I did something to deserve it. The only damage it did was cause a temporarily bruised ego and a little reddening of the behind. I admit I earned the strap on a few occasions. It did me far more good than it ever did me harm.

Oh, so many fond memories. I have shared but a few here. If only this could be my permanent home, my family.

The stability of four years came to sudden end in May 1960, when I was abruptly removed from the Monshors' home. I would, as you see in the following chapter, be placed in yet another foster home (#11).

I remember that fateful day of May 17, 1960, like it was yesterday. We had celebrated Susan's sixteenth birthday two days previously. I scampered through the alley from school heading home.

Upon entry into the backyard, I saw Mom. She was crying. She came to me and held me. I looked up and could see inside the enclosed back porch what had to be a social worker. Without a word being said, I knew then why Mom was crying. I was again going to be taken from the only ones I ever called Mom and Dad.

I broke down crying as Mom held me tightly. I tried as best as a ten-year-old could to reassure Mom. I told her, "It's okay, Mom, I'll be all right. No matter where they send me, you'll always be Mom."

With that, I dried my eyes and went inside to "bag" my worldly possessions, not knowing what would be in store for me. I knew I had to be brave for Mom! I packed a just a few possessions in the bag and went out to the living room. There was Mom standing by the social worker still crying. She asked where all my other things were. I told her she might care for another little boy and I would want him to have them.

I, one more time, hugged Mom and told her I loved her and to tell Dad the same. With that, before starting to cry again, I told the social worker I was ready. I ended up being the last foster child Mom and Dad would care for.

As the social worker and I made our way to the front door I could still hear Mom crying. I had to keep walking. Throughout all this the social worker said nothing. Little did I know, I would never again be returned to Mom and Dad's home.

However, Catholic Charities didn't know I was already a very determined young boy and that they could not break the bond that had been established. Six and a half years of my ten years of life had been spent with the Monshors. They had cared for me and loved me; my feelings toward them could not and would not be changed.

The removal from their home did not end my relationship with Mom and Dad. You will read about them in following chapters about Foster Home #11, and my years at Boys Town. They are integral parts of those stories during those days, so I won't tell the stories now.

Let's jump ahead in years now from 1960 to 1968.

Upon my graduation from Boys Town in 1968, I was released as a ward of the court. I was considered an adult and able to do as I wished. I continued to write and visit Mom and Dad. Yes, though I had not lived with them for eight years, they still were Mom and Dad to me. I wrote them during my college years and as I went out in the world to make it on my own. I visited them whenever I could make my way to Detroit.

How well I remember my last visit when I saw Dad. He was sitting in the kitchen as the visit ended. I got down on my knees to give him a big hug and tell him that I loved him. He didn't seem to want to let go. When he finally did, I looked up at him and for the first time I can remember, I saw tears in his eyes.

Dad was not a very demonstrative man. That day he seemed to be telling me that he knew this would be the last time we would see each other. It was his way of saying good-bye and also that he loved me. I took him back in my arms to hug him once again, and to let him know I understood what he was saying and to repeat that I loved him. We both ended up in tears.

On October 15, 1975, Ernest Monshor (Dad) died at age 66.

Just eight short years later on April 24, 1983, Mildred Monshor (Mom) also passed away at age 71.

Mom and Dad never told me during their lives that they attempted to adopt me as their son. I would learn of this only after Mom's death, during the search for my birth parents.

If they could have told me, it would have eased the pain of my youth thinking that I was a child not wanted. I believe they, in their own protective way, thought they were again shielding me from hurt, and I don't hold their not telling me against them.

Mom and Dad had attempted to adopt me in early 1960. They were denied with no reason given. It was just weeks after that I was removed from their home. The record shows I was removed for alleged physical abuse by Mom. That is absolutely untrue…it never happened!

A couple years after Mom's passing I decided to write Sonny Monshor. I wanted to share some memories of Mom and Dad with him and also hoped to obtain some pictures of them and myself during my childhood years.

I had not heard from Sonny at this point for over a quarter of a century. I did not receive a reply to my letter to Sonny and thought that this would be the end of my story and relationship with the Monshors. I would be left alone in this world and just have my memories of them to cherish.

Eighteen years passed since that letter to Sonny. Many times as I have written chapters for my story I have thought of the Monshors and wanting to include them in my story. I had thought of writing to Sonny one more time…each time I responded with a "no." I did not want to get hurt again.

On April 15, 2003, I had a change of heart. For some reason I could no longer tell myself no. I wrote Sonny a short letter. I have to be honest and say I did not expect a reply.

I work nights. So I can sleep during the day, I turn the ringer of my phone off. Many days I leave it off after I awake so I am also not bothered by the bombardment of telemarketers. I let my answering machine screen calls. Well, many days I tend to forget to even look at my answering machine to see if there are any messages on it. I do this even though the machine is right next to my home computer and I am at it every day.

On Monday, April 21, 2003, after not checking my machine for a few days, I suddenly looked over at it. I saw there were two messages on it.

WOW! You could have blown me over with a feather when I listened to the first message. "Hi Larry, this is Sonny Monshor." There were a couple things in between, but it ended with, "Marge is with me, and she's still my gal." Memories of that Christmas night in 1953 (50 years prior) came flooding back again. I was overwhelmed and on cloud nine!

I didn't even listen to the second message on the machine. I immediately attempted to return Sonny's call. The line was busy and would remain so for the next half hour. Talk about the need for patience!

After the sixth attempt, I heard the phone ringing. Marge answered the phone and I asked for Sonny without identifying myself. I heard Marge yell out to Sonny, "I think it's *our* Larry!" She also came back to me saying, "It is Larry, isn't it?"

"Yes, Marge," I responded. My head was still spinning from the words.

"*Our Larry.*" *Our*. I had not talked with them in over forty years. My last time with them was in 1959 when Sonny got a job with NASA. They came to the house to say good-bye to the folks. I remember crying as I clung to Marge and Sonny and the two little girls I considered my nieces, Gayle and Maryann…forced to say good-bye to people I had grown to love.

Soon Sonny came to the phone. "Larry, how are you?" he said. It was like we had last spoken only yesterday, rather than 40+ years ago. Then without hesitation, the shocker of the call came.

I heard Sonny say, "Do you know *we* tried to adopt you?"

"Yes, I learned Mom and Dad tried to adopt me once," I said.

"No, not Mom and Dad…Marge and I," was the reply.

I was briefly stunned. "What do you mean?" I asked. Then out came yet another surprise.

"Mom and Dad tried to adopt you when you came back home in 1956. They were denied. When that happened, because Marge and I loved you so much also…we then tried to adopt you. We wanted you as part of *our* family. We saw how you loved Gayle and tried to be her big brother…and we wanted you to be."

"Oh my God, I never knew of Mom and Dad's first attempt and had no clue you ever tried. You aren't kidding me, are you?" That was my reply.

Sonny then shared how devastated Mom and Dad were when they were denied in their adoption attempt. They wanted so much for me to permanently be part of the family…and to be their *son*.

I now understood why the "son" stocking was hung on the fireplace that Christmas in 1956. Mom and Dad were hoping it would become true! Sonny and Marge had married in 1954. Marge had Gayle as her first born and then Maryann. They wanted a son as well as a big brother for the girls. I fit the role perfectly and they also loved me. I would also permanently be a part of the family, though Mom and Dad would then be called Grandma and Grandpa. Instead of having Sonny as a brother and Marge as a sister-in-law they hoped to become Mom and Dad. They were not approved and no reason was given.

I would have been happy and proud to call them Mom and Dad. I would have been able to call Sonny's parents Grandmother and Grandfather. A year later they made their move to Florida never to see or talk to me again until this day…44 years later!

I just found it so hard to believe, though I knew it was true, what Sonny was telling me. Not *once* but *three times* someone told the foster care system they wanted me as their son. Three times they denied the request. I kept going back to this as Sonny and I continued our lengthy conversation. It had to sink in. To think I was allowed to go through my childhood into my adult life thinking no one wanted me.

Maybe it is better I am just finding out today of these attempts to adopt me. I know I am better able to deal with the pain I feel now than I would have been able to as a six-year-old or eight-year-old and even as a ten-year-old. Now I know how untrue this feeling actually was. I knew I was loved and now I know I was wanted far more than I ever even imagined before.

Sonny and I, and Marge, as she was on a second line, talked about so many things as time rolled by. He recalled the story of Christmas 1953 as if it were just yesterday along with other memories. We talked about our lives since those days.

Marge, at one point, interjected how different I sounded. I had to remind her I was no longer the soprano-voiced nine-year-old she remembered, but now a man of fifty-three. I hope my voice had changed!

I brought up the subject of my letter of eighteen years prior. Yes, Sonny remembered getting it but never being able to reply to it. It was lost. They had hoped throughout these past years that I would write again so they could contact me. Here all these years I believed I had been rejected. Oh, so many lost years because of a simple misunderstanding!

Sonny told me that he couldn't remember how many times over the years that he and Marge had thought about me, how they had talked of me and wondered how I was, where I was and what I might be doing.

As I sit here writing this chapter, I think of the years I thought Sonny looked at me as just another of the foster kids Mom and Dad had in their home. I now find out that it was his heartfelt desire...if he couldn't have me as his brother...he wanted me as his *son*! What an awesome thought. I have chills running down my spine as I think of it. Oh, how wrong I had been.

There were many other thoughts shared during this conversation, but I choose to keep them within myself.

We ended our conversation, so grateful on all our parts that this day had finally come. We would write, talk on the phone and hopefully soon be able to see each other face to face again.

That night at work, despite the length of conversation, I wrote a long letter to Sonny and Marge. The one thing I remember saying was, "I would have been happy and proud to have been able to call you Mom and Dad." I enclosed with the letter pictures of me at eleven and eighteen along with more recent pictures. They can see me as the youth they remember, and now as the adult I have become.

The loss of forty-four years of sharing with Sonny, Marge, and the girls weighs heavily on my heart. The feeling of "what if" and "if only" repeats itself in my mind. *So* many opportunities lost; so many could-have-been memories never to be memories. How different my life might have turned out...though I will not sit here and complain.

Alas, I cannot dwell on what has happened as I do not have the ability to undo anything. Things have happened and are forever written in the chapters of our lives. But today, we are given a new opportunity to create a new chapter in this book of life. To create memories, to create sharing experiences and most importantly...to share the love that has always been there for each other. Now that we have found it, we will not let the opportunity for a second chance slip through our fingertips.

It is late afternoon of April 24, 2003, as I write this chapter, after having begun it earlier this morning. Today is the twentieth anniversary of Mom's death. Because of what has happened in these past few days and the experience in the early hours of this morning while at work, I can say I am now complete and at peace.

Shortly after midnight this morning I left my office desk and walked outside. I looked up at the stars; it was a very clear night out. As I looked above, I softly whispered a prayer of remembrance for Mom. I wanted to let her know I remembered and I still loved her.

Those that know me know I am not a religious man, at least not in the "church" sense. I am, however, a man of deep spiritual inner faith…it is what has gotten me thus far through life.

As I concluded my prayer, I felt a soft, warm breeze flow by me and soon I felt totally comforted and at peace. In my heart and soul I knew it was Mom from above letting me know that everything was all right. She was now at peace knowing her *sons* had once again come together. She, in some mysterious way, had helped bring this day about.

We were, though it will never be legally recognized, a *family* once again.

On the same day I wrote my letter to Sonny, I also wrote to a Genevieve Monshor. I believed this might be Sonny's adopted sister with whom I had spent six years of my childhood. When two weeks passed without an answer to the letter, I thought, I either have the wrong person or too many years have passed and she may not remember me. May 8, 2003, changed those thoughts. When I went to the mailbox there was a letter from Genevieve. On the outer flap of the envelope she wrote, "I have never forgotten." My hands trembled as I opened the letter. I share its content here with you.

Dear Larry,

I have been waiting for this day all my life. God, I can't believe I can be so happy. Today is my 55th birthday, what a birthday! You just don't know how much I have been praying for this. I have so much to say. I have always loved you. I still have no family. I guess some things are not meant to be. I am writing so fast, I want to write more but I want to get this in today's mail.

Love,
your sister Genevieve Monshor

P.S. Thank God...please write back

Though I wrote my letter to Genevieve on April 16, 2003, it was delayed and did not arrive until May 5, 2003...Genevieve's birthday! Rather than waiting for a letter to get to her, I immediately picked up the phone and called her. We spoke for an hour. She has her own story of sadness and hardship. She has had a very rough life. She has proven she is a survivor. I will keep her story to myself. However, our reconnection ended just as quickly as it began. This unfortunately was not the reunion I had hoped it would be.

One Monshor of my childhood, however, is missing from this reunion. Susan Monshor passed away on October 23, 2001, at the young age of fifty-seven. Susan was the oldest of the kids while I was with the Monshor family, when Sonny was away. Unfortunately, I have no memory of ever doing anything with her, but I do have a clear vision in my mind of what she looked like.

I have spent the past twenty years in the search of this peace within myself. I know that not only did someone love me, but also wanted me as a son. I found a degree of comfort, as you will see in future chapters of this book, in finding my birth parents, siblings and extended family...but nothing compares to the peace I had early this morning. I know now my long searching journey is over. I have found what I have been looking for these past many years. I am home, I have my family...I can ask no more of life.

My life has now come full circle. From the Monshor home full of love and acceptance, to many years of wandering in the wilderness of life not knowing if anyone cared, to home again with people I have always loved.

I know I will do other research, as the interest in genealogy is there. But the searches will be for genealogical purposes only…I have found *everything* else that I was searching for.

I know throughout my life, in a spiritual way, that I have not walked alone. In real life, many times I have felt I have…that feeling will be no more! It is fitting that this chapter was begun on April 24, 2003, the twentieth anniversary of Mom's passing…I don't believe it was just a coincidence it worked out this way.

Rest in peace, Dennis. Rest in peace, Dad. Rest in peace, Mom. Rest in peace, Susan. I'm home.

Now that I have shared Mom and Dad with you and moved across many years, we need to return to 1960 to continue the story I want to tell. We return to that fateful day when I was removed from Mom and Dad's for the third time and sent to the hellhole of my life.

A gathering of neighborhood kids to celebrate a birthday in 1954.
I am the "bowtie boy," age 4.

A Monshor family portrait in which I am included
as a part of the family taken in 1956:
Dad, Genevieve, baby Gayle, Mom, Susan and me.

Sonny and I celebrating the 4th of July in 1957 in the Monshor family backyard.

My final Christmas with the Monshor family in 1959:
Susan, Genevieve, Gayle and me.

Chapter Three

FOSTER HOME #11

The stability of four years came to a sudden end in May, 1960, when I was abruptly removed from the Monshor home. I was placed in the Wayne County, Michigan Youth Detention Center. My crime: at age ten I was guilty of not having a family to claim me as their son nor a place to call home.

The Detention Center was to be my home until a new foster home was found. Here I was placed amongst youth offenders who were charged with a wide assortment of crimes. I believe I was the youngest on my cellblock. My bed, due to overcrowding, would be a thin mattress in the open area of the block.

Here, I had to learn how to fight quickly. Being the youngest amongst those on my block, older youth assumed I would be an instant prey for their follies. I proved otherwise. Though I lost a few fights, I was soon left alone as some youth thought of me as the crazy boy, because I would fight whoever tried something with me no matter their size. I think I actually gained a little respect from the other youth since I would take no guff from anyone.

In July, another foster home was found...the eleventh in ten years. This is the only foster home experience I have any memory of, other than the three times with the Monshors.

The two homes were as different as night and day. How this home was ever approved as a foster home, I will never know. With the Monshors I was made to feel a part of the family, whereas at this home I feel I was considered a monthly stipend.

My bedroom was a cot out on the enclosed back porch. Because this was also the laundry room it was important that I put everything away first thing each morning. I was actually allowed to sleep in the house one night, when I got sunburned. I slept on the kitchen floor with a fan running to keep me cool. I was given an extra blanket during the winter months. However, it was still cold and most nights I also slept in my clothes to keep somewhat warm.

I was given one meal a day. This was dinner and it was expected to last me until the following night. I was not allowed to eat this one meal with the family. A plate was prepared for me to take out to the back porch to eat alone.

I was also expected to do my homework out on the porch after dinner then go to bed. The only time I was really allowed in the house was to use the bathroom facilities. I made sure I used them and would be out of the house before others began rising.

When school began in the fall I was expected to walk about a mile to and from school each day…and not through the best of neighborhoods. This was also despite the fact that both their son and daughter had cars and could have driven me to school.

I arrived at school most days quite hungry. This was in the days before school lunch programs. Here, I learned how to steal to take care of my hunger. I was going to a Catholic school and each school day started with mass. I began to arrive at mass a little later than the other students. Most left their lunches in the outer lobby. Because I didn't want anyone else to go hungry, I would sneak around to different lunches and steal different items so I too would have something to eat during the day. I never got caught. After all these years I still feel bad about having done this.

There was a Catholic church also close to this foster home. I went to mass one Saturday morning. An elderly priest offered the mass. I was the only boy in attendance. The priest stopped me that Saturday and asked me if I lived in the neighborhood and if I would like to be an altar boy for Saturday mass. I answered yes to both questions. Father took me out for breakfast after that mass and each and every Saturday thereafter. I now had a second meal on Saturday and didn't have to steal it.

I soon developed a habit on Saturdays where I would leave Father and find a way to run off to the Monshors and spend the rest of the day with them. They welcomed me with open arms. I would leave in time to get back to this home before dark. After a few weeks it was arranged with the Monshors to pick me up after breakfast with Father and then drop me back off at this home, parking a couple blocks away so no one would know. This foster family never asked where I spent my Saturday, though I would be gone all day. They didn't seem to care.

I remember Christmas 1960 with this family. A few weeks prior to Christmas, I was taken to St. Vincent de Paul Center to get my semiannual allotment of clothes. Those clothes were what I found under the tree for me that Christmas morning; there was nothing from the family.

I do not remember ever having a tender or loving moment with this family. I was not a part of it. I was just the foster care system's kid for whom they were providing a bed and a meal a day…that was the extent of it. I was to spend 8½ months in this hellhole.

On the night of April 15, 1961, I was told to pack my paper bag, and that I would be leaving in the morning. All I could think of was, "Here we go again."

The final insult of this foster home came on my final night there. Their son, seventeen at the time, came back on the porch late during the night. He nudged me roughly. When I opened my eyes, light was coming through the porch windows so I could see him. He was standing over me, exposing his genitals close to my mouth saying, "Take care of this for me." I remember kicking out at him and then wailing away at him. I hit him everywhere I possibly could create noises as he crashed into things. All the time I was yelling to arouse the rest of the house.

Finally his mother came out to see what was going on. I yelled out, with tears rolling down my face, "He tried to force himself on me sexually." He called me a liar and said he was just checking on me.

His mother believed him and not me. She said, "You are a rotten, good-for-nothing boy, a dirty little boy, a liar. No wonder no one wanted you as you aren't fit to have anyone to want you. Good thing you will soon be out of our house, you ungrateful little bastard." At least she got the bastard part correct.

I sat there in stunned silence with what I heard, while crying now uncontrollably. Then I had my chance. I stood up and decked her son. I got a good hit in as I knocked out one of his front teeth…not bad for a scrawny eleven-year-old.

Dawn was soon approaching. It couldn't come fast enough for me. I couldn't wait to get out of there. I remember being slapped hard across the face and told to go get my bag and get out of their house…to sit on the front porch until the case worker came for me. That suited me just fine! When the case worker arrived I ran for the car.

Unbeknownst to me, some time during the fall of 1960 the court must have determined that my constant moving was proving to be detrimental and that they needed to get me out of Detroit. They realized that wherever they sent me in Detroit, I would find a way to run away and go back to the Monshors.

Maybe they just wanted to admit they had failed me. Eleven years old and I had already been moved in and out of homes fourteen different times…eight of those moves in just the first five years of life. Another sign of their failure was that as far back as I could remember, each time a social worker came to where I was staying…it was a "new" social worker. Seems to me first the social workers gave up on me and finally the system.

Dawn April 16, 1961, I was taken from this foster home and placed on a plane with a social worker, not having been told where I was going. After a plane transfer in Chicago, we landed in Omaha, Nebraska, and were met by a priest. It was then I learned that I was going to Father Flanagan's Boys Home, better known as Boys Town, Nebraska. I had never been on a plane before, never been out of Detroit and now I was in some city called Omaha and I was scared to death.

I was so ashamed of what had happened that previous night that I did not share it with the social worker. I have not shared it with anyone as I have remained ashamed until now…forty-plus years later.

I always felt I needed to keep it as my dark, dirty secret. As I thought of writing this chapter, I finally came to realize I was not the guilty party that night. I was the victim and thus could now forgive myself and let it go. I still obviously remember that woman's final words to me. I still shudder when I think of this foster home.

I have tried to get as many records from the court as I could. Most of them are stored on microfiche. What has been stated here and in the previous chapters was obtained from the application the social worker filled out for my admission to Boys Town.

However, back in 1986, a then current administrator did go through some of the microfiche to see if she could find any behavioral or medical problems on my part, which may have precluded me ever being adopted. She found none. She also could not find any reason for so many moves. The only thing she could figure out was that as I grew older I became less acceptable to couples looking to adopt. This problem continues to plague older, foster care children today. I have very few vivid memories of my childhood. It mostly seems a blur to me except for what I have shared.

The move to Boys Town would be the fourteenth move in my eleven years of life.

Chapter Four

BOYS TOWN GRADE SCHOOL

I arrived at Boys Town, Nebraska, in the late morning of April 16, 1961. A priest from Boys Town had met my social worker and me at Eppley Airport in Omaha and drove us the miles to the Boys Town campus. At the time, Boys Town was 10 miles west of Omaha. Today Omaha surrounds the campus.

I arrived, a terrified boy of eleven. I had "my bag" of worldly possessions with me. I had no idea what was to become of me. I was in a place I had never heard of before arriving.

After a brief meeting with a caseworker, my social worker departed Boys Town for her return flight to Detroit. I felt I was alone and lost in the world.

I was taken to what they, at that time, called the Orientation Center. There, I was shown a bed and a locker that was to be mine supposedly for the next 2-3 weeks. Then I was tested, interviewed and they determined to what part of Boys Town I would be sent.

I still very clearly remember crying myself to sleep my first night at Boys Town and for nights afterwards.

Boys Town at the time was divided into a grade school section and high school section. Grade school boys, such as me, were sent to one of four dormitory-styled buildings after orientation. Each building had four dorms holding 25 boys. Each boy was assigned a bed and a locker.

Part of the testing program in orientation was that each boy who came through was taken to what was called the choir section, to be voice tested to see if they had a voice that might have choir potential. Apparently I did, as after orientation I was assigned to Gregory Hall, in which only choir members were assigned.

I still remember after being at Boys Town about a week, a counselor coming to visit with me. While talking with me he decided to check out my locker.

There he found "my bag." I should say that in the first days there one was taken to the clothing store on campus and given a number of sets of clothes and toiletries. Mine were all packed in "my bag."

The counselor asked me, "Why are all your things in a bag rather than hanging up or on the shelves?"

I told him, "I wanted to be ready when they came to get me again to take me elsewhere."

The counselor called me over and took me in his arms, saying, "No one is going to come and take you away. I know about your life to this point and I want to let you know....you now have a home."

I don't think he ever fully figured out the emotions he triggered within me with those words. My eyes began misting up and before long I was crying uncontrollably. "You now have a home" kept going through my mind. "No one is going to come and take you away." For the first time in my life someone had actually said "You are home." I had waited over eleven years to hear those words. I don't know how long the counselor held me in his arms, but I know it was long enough for us to miss dinner in the dining hall and he had to make arrangements for food to be brought to me. I know that for the first night since coming to Boys Town I did not need to cry myself to sleep.

Soon after leaving orientation for Gregory Hall, I was caught up in the activities at Boys Town as most boys were. Though the school year would soon be over, I was assigned to the 5th grade. I began daily choir practices along with the other choir members. Now that I had a home, my life looked different. I even unpacked "my bag" for the first time in almost eleven years...it was never packed again.

Each boy at Boys Town was allowed to have an approved mailing/visitor list. I submitted only one family's name: the

Monshors. I might be over 800 miles away from them, but I still considered them my parents. I could only hope they would be approved, as I did not know if the court would tell Boys Town not to allow any further contact with them. Fortunately there was no court order and they were approved to write and visit. I wrote them long letters every week telling them of "my home." They promised to make the trip to Nebraska for Christmas to visit me.

Christmas 1961 was my first of seven Christmases at Boys Town. The Monshors kept their word and did come to visit the Sunday prior to Christmas. It would turn out to be the only trip they were able to make to Boys Town. The following spring Ernest suffered a heart attack that would limit his abilities from then until his death in 1975.

Because of the long bus journey to and from Boys Town, they were only able to stay for a few hours. They saw to it that I would find presents from them under the tree come Christmas Day. I remember standing at the Boys Town Pylon as they boarded their bus to travel back to Omaha to catch the Greyhound to Detroit....crying because I wanted to go with them.

Christmas is the highlight of the year for most boys there. It starts actually with all the boys attending Midnight Mass followed by hot chocolate and donuts at the dining hall. Upon the return to our respective dorms, Father Wegner, then the Director of Boys Town, came by each dorm to give out Christmas presents. Boys Town made sure no boy was forgotten at Christmas, even if they had no family to remember them. Each boy was given a gift and a large stocking full of candy, nuts, fruit, and other stocking stuffers. Christmas Day brought a holiday meal with all the trimmings. Despite all Boys Town offered this holiday, it left me with an empty feeling. Yes, I now had a "home." Yes, the Monshors considered me a son adopted or not. Still loneliness filled me as I felt so alone. For the first time in months I cried myself to sleep early that first Christmas morning. I would rarely celebrate Christmas again during my remaining six years at Boys Town.

One year I did celebrate was during my 7th grade year...didn't want to but was more or less forced to do it. Boys Town used to have what was called "Twelve Nights" during the holidays. Each day brought some new activity. On December 26th, St. Stephan the martyr was commemorated. A boy was chosen as the St. Stephan and he chose his protectors. He was allowed for a period of hours to give orders to anyone and they had to be obeyed. Of course his day ended by him and his protectors defending themselves in a snowball fight. This particular year I was chosen...doubt it was for popularity reasons. I have to admit, I had fun for the day.

The remainders of my middle school years were rather uneventful. I continued to pass to my next grade. I was singing in the Chancel Choir and later the Repertoire Choir and Concert Choirs. During those years, I did not consider myself very athletic, so I left sports alone. I was awaiting graduation from eighth grade when I would be able to transfer to the high school section and a new world of privileges would await me.

Though Boys Town was considered a village unto itself, it was very much a part of the Omaha community. Because I was active in choir and other music programs, I had many opportunities to travel into Omaha with an escort, to attend a wide variety of functions. These events could include chamber music concerts, chorale concerts, or even us boys giving concerts.

Boys Town also had a wide-ranging athletic program, and back in the 1960s we were amongst the top teams in the state. Boys Town won several state titles in basketball and football. When the teams were not playing at home, we boys went to town with them to cheer them on. Thus, many opportunities presented themselves for us to meet people of the community and even develop friendships. Most of my friendships came while I was in high school, but I loved the chance to go to Omaha for events while still in grade school.

They found I had a voice. I was a member of the famous Boys Town Choir 1961 through 1968.

Chapter Five

BOYS TOWN HIGH SCHOOL

June 1964...Grade School Graduation Day. I am now in high school. Graduation Day is the day any boy who had spent some years at Boys Town awaited. I had already been here over three years. I would move from a dorm of 25 boys to a cottage that had 5 bedrooms with only 4 boys per bedroom. Privileges not allowed grade school boys were now mine; I could obtain passes to downtown Omaha; I could get a one-week vacation away from the home if I had somewhere to go and it was approved; I could start to smoke. Yes, Boys Town allowed high school boys to smoke back then. Now smoking is not permitted by anyone on campus.

Graduation was another one of those sad days for me. Many of the boys in my class of 1964 had family come to cheer their graduation. I had no one present.

Freshmen were allowed one pass a month to Omaha lasting for two hours. I remember my first pass. I had not been outside of the Boys Town grounds on my own since my arrival over three years earlier. We were taken by school bus to the downtown Greyhound terminal; this is also where we were picked up. I had nowhere to go and just walked for the two hours around downtown in amazement of all the buildings. I did stop at a place called "Kings" and had a coke and cheese frenchie and then it was back to Boys Town for another month. As one went through high school the time allowed and frequency of passes increased. Seniors could go every Saturday for eight hours. On future passes I found much more to do than the first trip.

During my first summer in the high school section I requested a vacation to be able to return to Detroit to visit the Monshors. They had already said yes! The request came back DENIED. I spent that first summer of high school on campus as other boys were allowed to go on vacations to families. I felt yet another arrow piercing my heart.

I felt a little athletic my freshman year and went out for wrestling and track. My wrestling career didn't last long, as after my first two defeats, the coach decided it was not my sport and suggested I concentrate on track. I ran hurdles and one mile. I was not spectacular at either, but survived the season.

I have to be honest and say I did not set the world of schooling on fire during my freshman and sophomore years of high school. As a matter of fact, I had no real interest in school and did only what was required to skate through. By the end of my sophomore year I ranked near the bottom of my class. It was not due to lack of intelligence, rather "I just didn't care."

At the end of my sophomore year I again requested a week vacation with the Monshors. Once again the request came back DENIED! I was furious and determined I was going whether it was approved or not.

A local family had befriended me during the past year. They had a son (Andy) the same age as I. They lived only a few miles from Boys Town. On a Saturday afternoon during the middle of the summer I ran into the farm fields surrounding Boys Town and then made my way to their house. I admit I lied to Andy's parents and said the visit was approved. I spent the afternoon playing with Andy. Towards the evening his parents thought I should get back to Boys Town and offered to drive me there. I again lied and said I needed to go downtown to catch the bus back. They believed me and thus drove me to the Greyhound terminal downtown.

They did not know that in my pocket I had $30.00, which I had saved from my job at Boys Town; each high school boy has a job to earn income while he is there. The $30.00 was enough for a one-way bus ticket to Detroit and one simple meal during the thirty-one-hour ride. Fortunately I knew I could make a collect call to the Monshors. I called them and told them I was on my way.

Though I was angry with them at first, I did realize that they would have to contact the court. I also knew Boys Town would call the court and report me as a runaway. Even if they hadn't called them I knew from the past that their home would be the first place they would come and look for me. It didn't deter me. I was determined to have vacation time with "my family."

The Monshors, rather than a court officer, picked me up at the bus station. They had worked out an agreement with the court to let me stay with them for a few days and they would convince me to return to Boys Town on my own. Boys Town had also already agreed to take me back. I spent three glorious days "at home." During this time Mom convinced me that Boys Town was, for now, the best place for me. I could finish my high school education and in two years I would turn eighteen and be an adult. At eighteen I would no longer be a ward of the court and I would be free to make my own decisions. With tears I reluctantly agreed.

A bus ticket was purchased and I was given money to have more than one meal on the return trip. Upon arriving in Omaha the same priest who greeted me over five years earlier once again greeted me and drove me back to Boys Town. I didn't even lose any privileges for my escapade.

My junior year brought a sudden transformation of my life that I am grateful for to this very day. I, even as a small child, loved to argue. If it were night I would argue it was day, anything for an argument. My English teacher that year was a Ms. Genevieve Condon. Yes, I even argued in her class! She saw something positive in my argumentative nature. Ms. Condon kept me after school one day early in the school year. She talked to me about my arguing and how she saw it as ability, if it were directed in the proper way. I had no idea what she was talking about.

Ms. Condon took me to meet Mr. Clarence Weinerth, another English teacher but also the coach for the newly begun Speech & Debate Team. Ms. Condon simply told him, "I think we have a debater for you." Yeah, I could now argue, and get away with it! Mr. Weinerth of course let me know that with the ability to argue I also now had to prove my case. This meant lots of hard work researching the question being debated. It also meant that to be part of the debate team and go to tournaments, my grades had to improve. I was determined to do whatever it took.

I made the novice debate team that year. I was a good debater, even though rough around the edges.

My senior year, I made the varsity debate team. My partner (Jim Acklin) and I were, if I say so myself, great. Jim and I were rarely defeated. We traveled throughout the Midwest on weekends during the season, accumulating numerous trophies as winners of the tournaments. Our record at the end of the season was 289 wins as opposed to only 29 defeats.

Mr. Weinerth this year also encouraged me to enter the Original Oratory competition. His advice was to write a speech on a subject I knew best. I wrote a speech on my childhood and how the system needed to change. It was an emotional, wrenching experience to write and each time I presented it in competition. I won numerous competitions.

Jim and I were featured almost every month during our senior year in the *Boys Town Times* monthly newspaper because of our accomplishments.

At one tournament a feature writer for the *Omaha World Herald* wanted to do a piece on debate and chose to sit in on a debate in which Jim and I were participating. The following Saturday, there we were on the front page, picture and all! Of course the high school principal had to blow up the article and plaster it on the trophy case. Because of the caption under my picture, I soon became known as the "Show Me Statistics" man.

In part the article stated:

No Crowds For Debates
Competition Is Keen Between Teams

There are no cheering spectators crowded in the gallery. Usually there are only six people in the room. But the determination of the competition could not be stronger.

This is debate, the "sport" that requires rigorous exercise of the mind, quick flexibility of attack and careful use of words.

As teams from Boys Town and St. John in Elkhorn paired off at a debate tournament at Creighton Prep last weekend, only a judge and a timekeeper were in the room.

The boys, Larry Adams and Jim Acklin from Boys Town, and Mark Theisen and Leo Victora from St. John, arranged their weapons. Each team had brief cases filled with books and pamphlets and a legal notepad. Each also had a large box filled with cards on which were carefully typed quotes, statistics and facts to support arguments.

The St. John team drew the affirmative argument: "Resolved: That Congress should establish uniform regulations to control criminal investigation procedures."

The Boys Town team would try to show that the status quo was best.

As one team spoke, the other took notes, discussed the best combating arguments and scrambled through quote cards to find the right one. As they finished there was a quick handshake.

They would have to wait several hours before the results were posted on a bulletin board, which showed that Boys Town had won.

Jim and Larry ended up going undefeated during the tournament and taking the tournament championship. Larry was chosen outstanding speaker.

Through my interest in debate I was introduced to Mr. Bill Wehbey who was attempting to start a Model United Nations program at Boys Town, as were other high schools around the country.

I agreed to participate only if I could choose the country I represented. He agreed. At this time, the 1967 war between Israel and Egypt had just concluded. I wanted to be the representative for Egypt. There was many a debate that year in our Model United Nations. I even won a vote in support of Egypt. Of course some years later, the two countries would make peace with each other, so I am proud of what I did back then.

In January of 1968, I decided to enter the political arena and run for Mayor of Boys Town. Boys Town is a separate village. When Fr. Flanagan began the home, he determined it should be self-governed by the boys themselves, of course with his guidance. A new mayor and city council would be elected every six months. I felt I had something to offer Boys Town and tossed my hat in the ring.

Campaign for Mayor is not a long, drawn-out campaign as we know them today. On election night the student body gathers in the Music Hall Auditorium and hears why each candidate wants to be mayor. Students then go to the polls and before bedtime you knew who the new mayor was. Unfortunately, over the years after Fr. Flanagan's death, these positions became popularity contests and did not have much influence in running the home. Football players were the most popular on campus, and needless to say my first venture into politics turned into a solid defeat, coming in next to last. It was not to be my last political venture.

In February of 1968, I turned eighteen. It was also my senior year in high school. Though I could have walked out of Boys Town, I didn't! I wanted to earn my diploma! It was also proving to be the first time in my life that I was accomplishing something and I wanted to see it to the end. I think in many ways it was the year I grew up!

A lot of things are packed into the last few months of a senior year. Boys Town was no different. In February, I was shocked to learn that my girlfriend (Marilyn) and I were chosen as king and queen of the Sweetheart Ball for Valentine's Day. Marilyn was a debater at another local high school. We had met at a tournament and started dating late in my junior year. I spent most of my passes into town my senior year, when I wasn't away at a debate tournament with Marilyn. We continued to date during my first years of college then things changed...more on that in the next chapter.

In April was an Awards Banquet for varsity athletes to receive their BT letters and jackets; debate was considered a sport at Boys Town and I wore my jacket proudly.

In May it was the Junior/Senior Prom at Peony Park Pavilion in Omaha. I wore a tuxedo for the very first time and of course took Marilyn as my date. Graduation but a few weeks away, we were allowed to stay off campus well into the night. Preparations also had to be made as to what I would do after graduation.

There is an Award Ceremony the Friday prior to graduation at Boys Town. It is when individual seniors are recognized for their accomplishments while at the home. I received two awards that day. The awards were $50.00 savings bonds, which matured not too many years ago. I was recognized as Debater of the Year and to my and everyone's amazement, I was named "Most Scholastically Improved Senior"!

Two years before I was near the bottom of my class of one hundred thirty-eight. Now I was in the top 5%. Ms. Condon and Mr. Weinerth had accomplished their mission. They took a poor student who loved to argue and made a winning debater/orator out of him while also for the first time giving him a genuine interest in school. I will forever be grateful to them both.

Ms. Condon is long deceased. I had visited Mr. Weinerth in my few return visits to Boys Town. He passed away at 95 in June 1999.

Though in his later years he was physically incapacitated, his mind remained as sharp as a knife.

On my last visit he had me take a scrapbook from his night stand to look at, one of the few mementos he took to the home with him. Inside were all the pictures taken and articles written of Jim and me.

His words: "I have always been proud of my boys." My debate partner Jim and I remained close friends after leaving Boys Town.

June 4, 1968, Graduation Day arrives. The day I had been awaiting for seven years, one month, and nineteen days.

Graduation at Boys Town is different from any other high school graduation in the country. You are not only graduating high school; you are also losing "your home."

Boys Town had for over seven years provided me a home. It had provided me nurturing, a spiritual compass and an education. Graduation meant you are now an adult and it is time for you to go out in the world and make whatever mark on it you are capable of. It meant that for the first time in over seven years I would once again be "homeless."

The graduation ceremony began mid afternoon on a Sunday and the rule was that *all* graduates must be off campus by 5 p.m. It was time to make room for new boys.

A day like graduation should be a joyous occasion as you have accomplished the first major step in your life. However, it was not such for me. I had made many friends in the Omaha and surrounding communities over the years due to debate, and many of them accepted my invitation to graduation. They cheered and stomped when my name was called. I still felt emptiness. Yes, I had friends present, but no family who would hug, congratulate and say how proud of me they were.

The fullness of graduation hit me after the ceremony when I walked to the high school building for the final time as a boy of Boys Town. After turning in my cap and gown I went to the table where I would collect a one-way bus ticket to wherever I wanted to go, $50.00 from Boys Town and whatever money I had saved during my years there...which came to about $700. Fortunately I had been a saver at Boys Town, a trait I still possess today. With a final good-bye and a wish of good luck it was time to go; time to "leave home." The only good thing was that this time I was not leaving home with only "a bag." I was leaving with suitcases of clothes, boxes of books and mementos collected over seven years.

I remember standing outside the high school building and wondering, "Am I ready?" "What am I going to do?" "Where is home?" and though I made sure no one could see, a mist blurred my vision.

I should note that on the Friday before graduation I learned I had two scholarship offers to continue my education. I accepted the offer from Midland Lutheran College in Fremont, Nebraska, over Henry Ford Community College in Dearborn, Michigan.

The Monshors for the rest of their lives never fully understood why I made the decision I did. They didn't understand that I accepted the fact that one day they would be gone and I would once again have to deal with no family. It was better to accept and deal with it at eighteen rather than later in life. I needed to make it on my own. This is what Boys Town had taught me to do. I could write them, I could now visit them, but I had to make my own way.

Ready or not it was time to leave from the safe, stable confines of Boys Town, which I had known as "home" into the world of the unknown.

Marilyn and I attend my senior prom at Peony Park in 1968.

Jim and me at a dinner given in our honor for an outstanding debate season in 1968.

Class Picture 1968

The following appears after this picture: Adams, Lawrence, Philip: Detroit, Michigan. Arrived at Boys Town April 16, 1961. Academic Course. Major letter: debate 4; Minor letters: debate 3, track 1, wrestling 1; Choir 1-2-3-4; Concert Band 1; String Groups 1-2-3-4; B Club 4; Knights of the Altar 1-2-3-4; Student paper 4.

Chapter Six

JAMES TIMOTHY ACKLIN
DEBATE PARTNER, FRIEND, BROTHER

I did not get to know Jim until my junior year of high school, though we had arrived at Boys Town just months apart from each other. Until my junior year, Jim and I traveled in different worlds. He was the one who cared about his school work and making something of himself. I, on the other hand, was just doing enough in school to get by.

Jim was already a varsity debater when I joined the team as a novice in the fall of 1966. He had been the first to join the debate team, when Mr. Weinerth decided to begin one. We did not get to know each other that first year on the debate team, but that would change the following year.

In the fall of 1967, Mr. Weinerth decided to pair Jim and me as partners, as he said, "I feel my best two debaters should be a team." The decision of Mr. Weinerth had a profound affect on my life that year and continues to this day.

For Jim and me that last year at Boys Town for both of us, we not only became debate partners but also friends. It was a friendship that would last until his untimely death.

Because the debate team spent so much time together preparing for tournaments and also many Friday nights at hotels during weekend tournaments, Jim and I were able to share our stories with each other.

Jim came to Boys Town in the fall of 1961. Jim had gotten in trouble with the law after the divorce of his parents. He regretted his mistake and took it upon himself to make his parents proud of him...to negate his mistake of the past. Through his years at Boys Town he was often troubled by the fact that his parents sent him away...he was many times in pain.

Jim taught me the importance of studying. He taught me that in order to be a good debater it was important to work, to do the necessary research on the question, to practice speaking. His teachings I am sure played an important role in my moving from near the bottom scholastically in my class to the top 5% in one year.

Jim and I were to win a whirlwind of tournaments in the year we were together as partners. We achieved a record that has not been matched in the 35 years since our graduation.

As I mentioned previously, I did not celebrate Christmas after my first year at Boys Town, that is until 1967. Back then all of us boys attended Midnight Mass after which we went to the dining hall for hot chocolate and donuts. Jim and I met in the dining hall this early Christmas morning and decided to go to his cottage and gather some others to play cards.

Before going to play cards Jim pulled me aside and said he had something for me. He had a box, which I opened, and inside was a glass window piece with a teddy bear and a heart. The card said, "To a special and hopefully lifetime friend." Yes, I admit I cried as Jim and I hugged and wished each other a Merry Christmas as well as promised to remain friends for a lifetime. Many promise this sort of thing as they graduate high school, but it was a promise Jim and I would keep....we were more than classmates or friends, we were *brothers* in the City of Little Men! The "gift" from Jim has survived 36 years and remains hanging in the center of the living room window wherever I have lived. It was the best Christmas I had of the seven I spent at Boys Town. Thinking of that Christmas all these years later still brings tears to my eyes.

Our time together at Boys Town would in months be coming to an end as we both prepared for graduation. Jim would receive a scholarship to the University of Notre Dame, while I received mine for Midland Lutheran College. Jim finished 2nd academically in our class of 134. I couldn't have imagined anyone doing better than Jim, but one fellow classmate narrowed Jim out for the top spot.

As Jim and I went our separate ways to college, I knew that there went a young man who would make his mark on the world, would not only make his father proud, but also all of us who ever had the privilege to know him during his years at Boys Town. Jim proved me correct!

While at Notre Dame Jim majored in sociology and joined the U.S. Air Force ROTC. He would also meet the future love of his life: Rose. Jim and Rose would ask Msgr. Nicholas H. Wegner, Director of Boys Town during our years, to perform their wedding ceremony.

Upon his graduation from Notre Dame Jim began a career in the U.S. Air Force. He was to serve as a B-52 pilot instructor at Griffins Air Base in Rome, New York. When the Air Force introduced the B-1B bomber, Jim wanted to be part of the program and became the 5th pilot trained to fly the bomber. He was to become one of Strategic Air Command's most experienced B-1B pilots with 280 hours of flight on that tragic day of his death.

On that fateful day in September, 1987, Jim, along with 4 other Air Force officers, were on a training mission over Colorado when the plane was hit by a large bird piercing the skin of the right wing. The bird shredded a high-pressure hydraulic line. As the instructor, Jim immediately took the controls of the plane. The plane had lost engine #3 and engine #4 was also damaged. There were 3 on the plane who were strapped in to ejection seats, including Jim, while the other 2 would have to don parachutes and jump...the plane was descending and shaking violently. As the plane went into its final dive Jim gave the order for his men to eject. The other 2 in ejection seats made it out safely but for some reason Jim's failed and he died in the aircraft with the 2 crew members who were unable to jump from the plane. It took two minutes from the bird hitting the plane until in crashed into the Colorado range land.

Boys Town and the nation lost a hero that September day. I lost a friend, a brother. I learned of Jim's death a few weeks after his death in a wonderful letter from his widow Rose. She shared the story of Jim's death with me as well as thanked me for being Jim's friend in the years that followed Boys Town…little did she realize that I should be the one doing the thanking for Jim's friendship and the bond that remained with us for 20 years. Jim, in addition to Rose, left behind two sons and thousands who will forever remember him and cherish the memories they have of him.

Two stories have been shared with me since Jim's death.

Apparently former Vice President Dan Quayle spoke of Jim during a visit to Boys Town in 1990. As told to me he said, "Jim was a hero. Jim was an example of a man who took responsibility for his life. Like Jim Acklin, so many of those before you here at Boys Town have chosen to serve your country and have chosen to make the sacrifice in the name of the cause of freedom." I didn't often agree with Quayle, but on the point of Jim being a hero…I sure did! The second comes from a letter Rose received after Jim's death from Brig. General Alan Rogers, Jim's Commanding Officer at Dyes Air Base in Abilene, Texas. He wrote:

> *Jim was a marvelous officer, instructor pilot and outstanding professional. He truly shaped and built the B-1B CCTS (Combat Crew Training Squadron). His skilled hand and keen mind will live through the excellence that he imparted to his students. No finer pilot flew the B-1B than Jim Acklin! He was an aviation pioneer who made a great contribution to our nation's defense.*

Jim, my debate partner, but more importantly friend/brother, has been gone since 1987. I think of him often. I think of the times we shared together in hotel rooms as we participated in debate tournaments, of how we laughed as well as cried during some of those times. I think of the many debates themselves that we did and how we both hated to lose, even though we rarely did. I think most of all of the friendship that began as young men of 17 and it endured so much during the twenty years that followed. I miss Jim and I always will.

Rose and I stayed in touch in the early years after Jim's death, but as time passed I believe the pain of memories was too much for her and we drifted apart so she might move on with her life. She and Jim's children, now both adults, I hope know that many remember Jim as friend, brother and hero and share in the pain they suffered with his loss.

Labor Day weekend 2002 I traveled to Boys Town. While there I visited the Hall of History. Within the Hall is a tower of brass plates *In Memorium* to former staff and boys of Boys Town. I noticed there was no plate for Jim. I could not allow Jim to not be a part of that tower...thus a brass plate has now been placed in Jim's memory so that he will continue to live on in the history of Boys Town, long after he and I are both gone from this earth. As long as Boys Town remains so too will Jim's memory! Jim is gone...but not forgotten. He remains a part of my life in my mind, heart and soul!

James Timothy Acklin speaks during a debate.

Chapter Seven

COLLEGE/ACCEPTANCE

On June 4, 1968, I was a young man of Boys Town. On June 5, 1968, I was a young man on my own.

I took my one-way bus ticket and returned for a visit to the Monshors in Detroit. During this trip Robert Kennedy was shot and killed in Los Angeles. "Bobby" had visited Boys Town just days prior to my graduation. His assassination brought back memories of hearing of John Kennedy's assassination while I sat in an 8th grade science class at Boys Town, how we were rushed immediately to the chapel to pray for our president and after his death, how we all sat silently watching the events unfold on a small black-and-white television screen. Only two months prior, Dr. Martin Luther King was also assassinated. THIS WAS THE WORLD BOYS TOWN SENT ME OUT INTO!

After returning to Omaha to work for the summer at a local Ford dealer, a classmate of mine (Renato) and I decided to get an apartment together for the summer. I couldn't really call it an apartment as it really was a dump! It contained a kitchen of decent size, a bathroom and a semi-large room that a divider had been placed down the middle of to make a small living room and smaller bedroom. It came furnished with old furniture. This we were to call "home" for the summer. We both spent as little time as possible there.

In August 1968, I had second thoughts about college and attempted to enlist in the U.S. Army, thinking it would be a better place for me as it provided a degree of regimen that Boys Town had. I did not feel comfortable having the total freedom I had desired…some say I was "institutionalized."

I passed all the tests prior to induction and was told to report the following Monday for my physical and departure to boot camp. The physical went smoothly, as I was in good shape for an eighteen-year-old, until it came to my eye exam. I failed the eye test. I had been born with a "lazy eye," meaning it roamed, but also, I was born for, all intents and purposes, legally blind in that eye…left (now 20/400). I was reclassified and told to go back to what I had planned as my services would not be needed…thus ended my almost military career.

As a child I had five surgeries on my left eye in an attempt to correct it. I have no memory of the surgeries but they are part of my records. I do remember, however, at 5 and 6 years old having to wear a patch over my "good eye" when watching television or reading at night for an hour in yet another attempt to correct it. It failed as the surgeries did.

I was warned early that due to the stress on the right eye because of the left eye problems, I would eventually see a diminishing of my right eye. This has proven to be true, as today my right eye is 20/200. I have started wearing bifocals, since without them, I would be totally unable to read or be at this computer composing this book. My vision seems to have stabilized now, but in time, further diminishment may occur…just another fact of life I may have to deal with. However, I digress.

I entered Midland Lutheran College in the fall of that year on a debate/cross country scholarship. I think the school either was confused or made an exception for me as though I had run track I had never competed in cross country.

I was off and running in college life. Within a few weeks of classes starting, I had decided to once again enter the political arena and run for Freshman Class President. You had to first get enough votes to be nominated and actually run a campaign. I did not receive enough votes to be placed on the ballot, but those who supported me insisted I run as a write-in candidate. I spent two weeks making signs, posting posters and talking to whomever I could stop and get to talk with me. I ended up losing in a very close vote. I decided maybe politics was not for me; thus, in just a matter of months, both my military and political careers came to an abrupt halt.

Two experiences stand out in my college career. The first happened within a month or so of my entering college. I received a phone call late one evening from a Mrs. Robert Wagner. She indicated she had been a foster parent who cared for me as a small youngster and had something that belonged to me. I told her that "parents' weekend" was coming up and if she wanted, she could come and visit me then…she readily agreed. I must tell you that I had no recollection whatsoever of her.

Mrs. Wagner arrived early on the Saturday afternoon of parents' weekend. She had a check for me in the amount of $1,000.00, which came from a savings bond bought for me when she and her husband cared for me and said it was rightfully mine.

Mrs. Wagner seemed rather distant and cold. She would only talk in the lobby of the dorm in which I was living and would not attend the football game. She spent only a few hours at school before arranging to return to Omaha to catch a plane back to Detroit.

I wrote her after her visit to thank her for the funds, which were much needed by me. I never heard from her again.

Years later, I found records indicating that she had been a "boarding parent," which means "foster parent." I have spoken to others just recently that have a different bend on the situation…which I tend to agree with.

I stayed with the Wagners for only 8 months at age 5. It is extremely unusual for foster parents to purchase a savings bond, unless an adoption was planned, while caring for a foster child. Also, I was now 18 and had not heard from the Wagners in 14 years. She also had to spend time in finding out what happened to me during those 14 years since I left her home, contact Catholic Social Services, Boys Town and finally Midland Lutheran College. No ordinary foster parent would go through all this. It is felt that the Wagners could have been prospective "adoptive parents," who, for whatever reason after a period of time, could not follow through on the adoption. However, after realizing I was now 18 and considered an adult she wanted to see for herself what happened to me, how I turned out. Once that was determined by her visit with me, her curiosity was satisfied and she was ready to move on.

The second experience that stands out of my college days: my needing to accept myself as the person I am! I had, as many young boys do, experimented with other boys, but never seriously considered myself a homosexual or gay, as it is called today. I had dated girls, and yes, I was sexually active in my senior year of high school.

However, a question of my sexual identity haunted me throughout my freshman and sophomore years of college. I was tormented by even the thought that I might possibly be gay...as I had been throughout my years at Boys Town, from time to time. I had to find the answer to the question: "Am I gay?"

In answering this question please let me make it clear...this is *not* an attempt to convince anyone on this subject...it is *my* answer! You have a right to disagree with me and I know many will...however, this is my story and not yours. Please respect my opinions as I will respect yours and your right to express them.

If you are heterosexual and reading this, stop and think: when did you decide you were heterosexual?

Was there a moment in your life when you said, "I will choose to be heterosexual," or did it come naturally? I believe if you are honest with yourself, you will answer there was no moment and that it just came naturally.

I believe I too was born who I am. I was born gay. Just as you cannot pinpoint a day or moment you made the decision to be heterosexual, neither did I wake one day and decide "I am going to be gay!" I did not choose to be gay...it came naturally...though I fought and battled it for many years until accepting who I was. In truthfulness I have thought I might be gay since I was seven...but did not accept it. It is not choosing to be gay that a gay person does...it is rather accepting yourself as a gay person!

Think for a moment: who in their right mind would choose to be gay considering the following:

- Being gay can mean a life of verbal insults and abuse by others.
- Being gay can mean being the subject of physical assaults.
- Being gay can mean death at the hands of another for simply being who you are.
- Being gay can mean the loss of a job or housing…it can't happen to you but it can to me!
- Being gay can mean rejection by your family and friends. My natural mother wished I would contract AIDS so I would die rather than she have a gay son.
- Being gay can mean being rejected by those who have never even taken the time to get to know you, except they have found out you are gay.

No, no one would choose to be gay considering the world that awaits them!

We do, however, in many cases, go through the struggle of accepting who we are. I did! Despite thinking at age seven I was gay, I rejected it. It went against anything I had been taught. Yes, I was raised that to be gay was wrong, it was a sin and it was sick.

I sought counseling and was told I wasn't gay, but only going through a phase and would grow out of it. Years later, I am still waiting to grow out of it. I was told I would meet the "right girl" and she would change me.

I was told by my parish priest I would be condemned to hell.

To make everyone happy, and I thought myself, I dated girls in high school and early years of college all the time knowing I might be lying to them, as well as myself. I came close to marrying one of those girls…what a life of hell I would have put her through if it had happened.

I remember the first time a fellow student called me a "fag"...it was like a dagger through the heart. I didn't want to be one of them!

I played sports and was active in many student activities, like other students....yet inside, I knew somehow I was different.

In 1970, at the age of 20, after years of struggle and torment, it all became too much for me to bear. I attempted suicide. I spent the night alone drinking "boilermakers" and "whiskey sours" to wash down the "pills." I went along until I overdosed, and went into convulsions and then lapsed into a coma. I was rushed to the hospital where they pumped my stomach. I lay in a coma for over two days, teetering on the brink of death. Suddenly, I came out of it.

The doctors indicated if my roommate had found me but ten minutes later than he did, I would have died there on the dorm room floor of alcohol poisoning and overdosing...as I had planned.

All the pain, hurt, confusion and torment that had been there before remained. Luckily, the therapist I went to afterwards understood where I had come from and where I was at in my life. Her words of "You are who you are, accept it...embrace it...be who you are" had an impact me. I will, however, never forget her other words, which changed my life: "Jesus loves you just as you are...you are what he created!"

I was born gay...all I had to do was accept who I was born as and live my life to reach the fullest of my potential and desires!

That was years ago. Six months later, I met the person who would become my partner for the next 22 years. I had what every person desires in life: a loving, caring, faithful relationship. As every couple, we worked, we paid our taxes and we tried to make our community better. The desires of life are no different for gays than that of heterosexuals. Unfortunately, as in some heterosexual relationships, my partner and I separated in 1992. Our story follows in the next chapter.

In the years that have passed, I have suffered verbal abuse, been physically assaulted and rejected by many. I have been preached against. I have had political leaders try to make me a second class citizen. I have felt the pain of seeing other gays killed...such as

Matthew Shepherd. I know of gay teens who have committed suicide. I have borne the sorrow of losing 141 of my friends, including some of my closest, to AIDS. Despite all this, though the scars borne of the past, have not, nor will not, ever completely heal...I am happy with who I am, where I am, and where I am going. I am now able to be honest about who I am, not only with others, but most importantly, with myself!

Just as many were born heterosexual, some of us were also born gay. We are no different from anyone, except for the gender of the partner with whom we share our beds. I have the same goals and desires that you do; a chance to live my life without fear, a loving partner to share my life with and to reach the fullest of my potential.

I ask for no special rights...just the same rights as any other person...to be accepted as a full member of the human race, with my good points, as well as my faults. Just as the late Dr. Martin Luther King asked, I too ask: "Judge me not on my sexual orientation, but on the content on my character."

Yes, this is my story, but it is also the story of millions of other gays and lesbians. They realize who they are, they struggle with it, they finally accept. They go about their lives, as does the rest of society, as best they can. Millions of us could walk down the street to work each day and you would never know we were gay unless you asked. We do not fit the stereotype image that the media, preachers and politicians have portrayed us to be. We are your sons, daughters, mothers, fathers, your next-door neighbors and friends. We come is all sizes, colors, religions and every walk of life. We ask only the same rights and protection of others, so we too may realize the dreams of our lives!

Resolving this issue in my life allowed me to finish my college career in 1972 with a degree, majoring in Business Administration. It was time for my partner and me to go make a life for ourselves.

Chapter Eight

MATT, LIFE PARTNER

I told the story in the previous chapter of my struggle with coming to terms with my being gay. This came about only after extreme turmoil within me and an attempted suicide. Finally, at age 20, I was able to accept myself as I was.

During the summer between my sophomore and junior years in college, I worked a local job. One evening I decided to go out to a gay bar. I had never been to a gay bar before. I remember driving around the block where the bar stood, a number of times before I even worked up the nerve to park the car. I sat there wanting to make sure I wasn't seen entering. Once I worked up the courage, I ran across the street to the bar as fast as I could...if anyone saw me I would be a blur. Back then in Nebraska, the legal drinking age was 19, so I was not involved in underage drinking.

I entered the bar, ordered a drink, and immediately headed for a corner. I wanted to observe, it was a whole new experience for me. I had never been in a place where gay/lesbian people gathered before. It did give me a good feeling knowing there were others in the world like me. I was not alone.

A short time after arriving at the bar Matt came up and introduced himself. He had noticed that I seemed somewhat fearful of being there. I should say Matt, at this time, had not turned 19 yet and should not have been in there, but you know how college towns are. We began talking. He was so easy to talk to. Though, as I have previously stated, I had experimented...I had never before been with a man sexually. I admit I was very much attracted to him. He stood 5'9", tall, black wavy hair, baby blue eyes and had a smile that would melt you.

After talking awhile he asked me to dance. I remember it was Gloria Gayner singing "I Will Survive"...how appropriate. Then a slow dance came on the jukebox and Matt asked me to continue dancing with him. I can't fully describe the feeling I had when we took each other in our arms. It felt so natural, so warm and so right for me.

We closed the bar that night and went out for coffee and talk. I didn't want the night to end. I told him of my struggle, of my fears and anything I could to just keep him with me. As dawn approached I finally worked up the courage to ask Matt to come home with me despite a fear of rejection. He accepted.

This happened on a Friday night. Matt and I ended up being inseparable that weekend. Monday morning I asked Matt to move in with me. Was it love at first sight or was it infatuation? It was probably the latter then, but oh, how I developed a deep love for him. As we went into the relationship and a circle of friends developed they were astounded by the fact we only were together a weekend before we moved in with each other. Many thought it would never survive, as so many gay relationships do not. Most gave it six months to a year. Boy, were we ever to prove them wrong.

I had always had a fear of relationships, as I had never experienced a relationship of any sort that lasted. My childhood was full of unfulfilled relationships. They always seemed to end before they got started. I did not trust others enough to completely open myself up to them, being afraid in the end that I would be hurt, as I had been so many times previously. I did not know what love meant nor how to be able to love someone. I don't think I fully loved myself at this point.

Matt changed all of that. Matt taught me to be able to love another person with heart, soul and every fiber of my being. He taught me to fully love myself at the same time. He was everything a person could ask for in a relationship.

A year into our relationship, we gathered friends to share in our commitment ceremony to each other. We promised to be together for better or for worse, sickness and in health, for richer or for poorer until death do we part. It was a solemn, sacred moment for me and a commitment I planned to do everything to keep.

In the following chapter you will see the road Matt and I traveled over the years together. We both worked, kept up our home, paid taxes, volunteered in the community to try and make it a better place. We wanted the same things and did exactly what a heterosexual couple would do within a marriage.

Matt and I were together not for six months or a year as some had predicted. We were together as a couple for 22 years. It was a committed relationship. We had our ups and downs as any couple would have. We made a promise to each other early in the relationship that if a problem arose, we would communicate until it was resolved. We also promised to never go to bed without saying "I love you," no matter how bad the day had been or if we had argued. We committed to be faithful to each other. At times, all these commitments were not easy, but we were both determined to do all the work necessary to make a relationship work. Yes, a relationship of any sort takes a willingness by both to work at making it work.

Unfortunately, as in marriages, all of this shattered in 1992, after having spent 22 years together, building a life together and feeling this would last a lifetime. There is one thing Matt and I said would always be unforgivable. That was for one or the other to be unfaithful in the relationship. For 22 years this never happened. Suddenly without any warning signs, Matt began being unfaithful. I had heard rumors but did not believe them...not after 22 years! I was away on a business trip and without notice came home from the trip early. Reality got thrown in my face. There was no discussion, no trying to work it out. Trust and a commitment had been broken and a promise earlier made had to be kept, as I have always tried to be a man of my word. I ended the relationship with Matt.

It is, to say the least, difficult to end a 22-year relationship with a person you loved so deeply. This was the person I had shared everything in my life with. He had shared the search and discovery of my birth parents. He had shared the deaths of so many friends with me. We had built so much together in those years, and as suddenly as it had begun, it was over. I was shattered. All the defenses that had been up about relationships with others were now back up to keep people at a distance. I did not want to open myself up to another person again, to make myself vulnerable, and to be hurt.

It took over four years before I could even begin to open up to others again, but even now, years later, I still keep them at a distance...I only allow them so close.

I do not hate Matt. I am thankful that we had 22 years to share together. Many gay couples do not have this opportunity. I am thankful for all he taught me about love, about myself and my capabilities. Matt did give much to me and hopefully I to him. I cannot say we have remained friends, as we have not. I have seen him from time to time over the past years. The meetings have been cool and distant.

I am single today because I choose to be, not willingly, but I fear opening myself up again as I once did. I am not a 20-year-old anymore. I survived one break-up and I don't think I have it within me to deal with another. I do, however, have a full life, am happy with myself and don't worry about whether there will be another person to share my life with or not. Life must go on!

Chapter Nine

NEW YORK, NEW YORK

Upon receiving my degree, my partner and I decided we wanted to move from Nebraska. We had heard so much about New York, though we had never been there. We both applied for jobs before the move. I landed a job as a Purchasing Agent for the Federal Bureau of Prisons Northeast District. In July 1972, we made our move. Even back then things were expensive in NYC. Based on our salaries of the time, we were only able to afford a "studio" in a brownstone on the upper west side of Manhattan. We paid then almost as much as I am paying for a two-bedroom condo today. It had one large room with a fireplace, a small kitchen and bathroom. Somehow we made a home of it, at least for a few years. We were on our way! We loved NYC in those early years. We took in all the sites, went to the theater, symphony and various other things NYC is so known for.

My partner and I both made advancements in our careers. We were able to move after a few years from our studio, to a one-bedroom apartment on 17th Street and 7th Avenue in Manhattan. We were coming up in the world.

I remained with the Federal Government until late 1978. I had advanced as far as I could at the time and did not want to wait for my superior to retire...I would still be waiting today!

I left my job and joined NYC government as Director of the Home Energy Assistance Program, provided energy assistance to the elderly and low-income populations. At this time Ed Koch was Mayor of NYC.

In 1980, Mayor Koch wanted to start a non-profit foundation to raise funds to provide meals to the elderly on weekends and holidays. This was due to the fact that Federal funding only provided meals Monday through Friday. If a person did not save food on Friday, unless they had family to provide meals, they went hungry until the next meals were delivered on Monday.

Mayor Koch asked my superior to recommend someone to head the foundation. She recommended me. When the mayor asked me if I would take the position, I agreed on the condition that I could also continue in my current position. Thus, I began wearing two hats. It was a grueling pace, but I thrived on it.

In a short time, we were able to raise funds to provide two meals a day on weekends and a grand meal on holidays for thousands of low-income elderly in all five boroughs of NYC. Today, the program is still going strong. It is called CityMeals-on-Wheels.

This year also brought tragedy into not only my partner's and my life, but also the nation. Early in the year, a new disease began spreading in the United States. It began within the gay community, but soon spread among IV drug users and heterosexuals as well. The disease was AIDS. It remains with us today and in the years that have passed since we lost our first close friend, we have lost 141 friends, including the 22 people closest to us in our lives. A special remembrance of them is included later in this book.

I'm a homeowner! In 1982, my partner and I were able to leave the rental market and purchase a condo in Brooklyn Heights. This is an upscale section of Brooklyn, just across the river from Manhattan. From it you could view the skyline of Manhattan. What a sight it was to view Manhattan at night from our living room window.

I was astounded in 1982, when I learned that Mayor Koch wanted me to submit papers for a nomination to the "White House Fellowship Program." This is a program where those who are accepted, go to Washington, DC for a year and work either at the White House or one of the cabinet departments.

Hundreds of nominations are submitted each year. Though I thought I didn't stand a chance of being chosen, I went through all the paperwork, background checks and interviews. Thirteen people are chosen each year for the Fellowship. Surprisingly, I made it to the next-to-last round of the selection process. I considered it an honor to just have someone feel I was worthy of nomination. I can only imagine how my life would have changed if I had been accepted into the program.

I do get to visit the White House! In late 1982, without my knowledge, Mayor Koch pulled another surprise on me. He nominated me for the District VI Presidential Volunteer Award for 1983. In the spring of 1983, mail arrived at my home bearing the seal of the President of the United States. It was an invitation to the White House to be the recipient of the award for which I had been nominated. I obviously went and received my certificate and plaque and had a brief time to confer with then President Reagan.

As a recipient of the award and because of why I received it, I was requested to present seminars the following day at the Marriott Hotel to Department of the Elderly Directors from across the country, as to how they could begin a CityMeals-on-Wheels program as we had in NYC.

In 1984, though I had already left the program, I was awarded the 1984 New York State Eleanor Roosevelt Volunteer Award for my work the four previous years.

In late 1983, I burned myself out in government. I think it was not only from my regular job, but also the fact that I was wearing two hats at once. I had also suffered my first heart attack not quite two years earlier, and felt I might be working my way towards another.

I took up a new position as a consultant to Polytechnic University's Alumni Association. The university is in Brooklyn Heights, not far from home. I created databases and analysis for them to improve fund raising from their alumni.

It is also at this time that an event that would forever change my life occurred...however, Chapter Ten is devoted to that story. Don't peek, finish this chapter first!

In 1986 my partner received an offer that would require moving from NYC. It would mean a move to San Francisco, California. We studied our options and realized we were both ready for a change. NYC had in the past few years become dirty and crime ridden, maybe San Francisco would be different.

Move west, young man! We sold our condo and made our move settling in an area of the city called Hayes Valley. It was close to Symphony Hall, Opera House, as well as fine restaurants and museums…just the things we enjoyed.

My partner had his job but I went out without one. I had been considering while doing consultant work at Polytechnic University that it would be great to begin my "own" consulting business. We figured now would be as good a time as any. Thus began the "LA Consulting Co."

Within a few months, I was able to obtain consulting contracts with Price Waterhouse San Francisco and The Canadian Consulate. It provided them with databases and analyses of how they could better their businesses. I worked this business hard for two years, but noticed that I was wearing myself out. The contracts were nice, but they were not large enough to allow me to hire help and I could not continue it on my own.

Fate would step in and resolve the problem for me. Again my partner had an opportunity to advance his career, which meant moving. We moved to Salt Lake City.

I completely changed the avenue of my career future. I joined a trucking company as an accountant. The owner of the company saw, after a while, that I was bored with just crunching numbers. He asked if I wanted to learn the trucking industry from the inside. I did! The rest is history, as I have been a part of the trucking industry since doing operations management there.

This career choice has taken me to Fargo, North Dakota, Phoenix, Arizona, a return to Fargo, North Dakota, and most recently, Dubuque, Iowa. It was a good career choice for me and I have never been happier in a job.

Before I conclude this chapter, I must say a very personal note in regard to the tragedy that befell our nation on September 11, 2001. Having lived in NYC for over 14 years, I was very familiar with the

World Trade Center. I had been to the Trade Center a number of times, and it also was part of the skyline I viewed every night during the latter years in NYC. This was not only an event I watched unfold on television, but was very, very personal to me.

A friend of more than twenty years and former coworker was among the 2,819 people to die in the Towers collapsing that day. He left behind a wife and two children.

It is difficult, having lived in NYC, to see pictures today without the Towers rising above all else in the city...they may rebuild, but it will never be the same!

I need to go back in time now. I said earlier that in 1982 a life-changing event occurred...one that is affecting my life until this day and will forever do so. It is time you hear that story!

Chapter Ten

SEARCH/DISCOVERY

As I have said in an earlier chapter, throughout my twenties, my concern was about my career, my life partner and the things any normal twenty-something would be concerned about.

I laid my childhood and adolescent years aside and hoped they would be memories of the past. I had hoped that those memories would stay locked up deep within me, never to reveal to anyone the heartaches they had caused. However, my life was soon about to change and never be the same again!

In May 1981, I was supposedly a very healthy man of thirty-one. The night before my life-changing event, I had jogged my usual three miles through the streets of Brooklyn Heights, New York, had eaten a healthy dinner and went to bed early enough to get the rest I needed.

The next morning I did my usual exercises before getting ready for work and felt great as I left for Manhattan. When I arrived at work, I had a meeting and suddenly found myself grabbing my chest and collapsing to the ground. I had suffered the first of three heart attacks.

Until that day I had not spent any time in the hospital since early childhood...for eye surgeries and to have my tonsils removed. One of the routine questions doctors ask is "What is your family medical history?" I was quite embarrassed to have to answer the question with an "I don't know." When I returned to health, I went on with my life and thought no more of the episode.

In the spring of 1982, my partner and I decided to travel to Greece for vacation. I needed a passport to do so, and to get it I needed my birth certificate. I knew where I was born...so I applied for it from the state of Michigan. In a few weeks it arrived. I was not ready for the impact this little piece of paper would have on my life until this very day.

On the certificate, I saw the name of a birth mother for the first time in my life: Roberta Adams. To see a mother's name blew me away. Could the story the Monshors had told me so many years ago be untrue? Could this name be made up by the nuns that supposedly found me in a dumpster? I continued reading the content of the certificate. It listed the hospital where I was born. It listed a home address for her. It gave her age of nineteen at the time of my birth, even gave a birth date! It even gave her place of birth. No father was listed. Finally it indicated I was her first born. The nuns just could not have made all this information up. For the first time since the Monshors had told me "the story" so many years ago, I had the sinking feeling it was untrue!

I made the decision at that moment...I must find this woman! I had to find out if in fact she was my birth mother. The questions began. Who is this woman? Why did she give me up for adoption? Is she alive? Does she think of me? Where is she? I remembered my heart attack of a year earlier and the question of what is her medical history? Is her or her family's medical history impacting me?

Upon my return from Greece, I began the search to get a few answers to those questions.

Little did I know of the process I was about to enter into. I went to the hospital where I was born...Providence Hospital in Detroit, Michigan. They would not release any records of the birth. I went to Catholic Charities, whom I was a ward of until my eighteenth birthday...they would not release any records. They said, "Forget the past, it doesn't matter."

I tried various organizations for almost three years, but to no avail. I scoured books that had to do with adoption and foster care for clues as to how I could do my research...again no answers. I thought

I was at a dead end and would never have the answers I was looking for.

Finally, in late 1985, the first big break I needed in my search came. I wrote to BOYS TOWN asking if they, through their records, could help me. They indicated since I was now an adult, I could have a copy of my records from my days at Boys Town and they sent them to me. What a treasure chest!

On the application form filled out by Catholic Charities twenty-four years earlier, they listed not only my mother's name but my father's name, Robert; my maternal grandparents John and Sarah and two aunts, Doris and Frances. They gave a description of my natural parents and what they were doing at the time of my birth, as well as that of my grandparents. I could not believe all that I was reading. I also saw for the first time that my last name should have been Piechowiak and my heritage is Polish.

I quickly remembered all the Polish jokes I told during my school days and even adulthood. I knew now that *yes*, I had a family out there somewhere and I had my *own* heritage. But this was only the beginning...how do I find them? I was determined they would be found!

I lived in New York City at the time. They have a great research library and I spent week upon week devouring records with no results. Finally, I decided, on a whim, to check Detroit phone books going back to the time of my birth, which the library had.

I did not find my birth parents, but found my grandparents. I tracked them in the phone books. My grandfather had a unique way of listing his name, from 1950 thru 1971. Suddenly they were gone. Had I reached another dead end?

On a second whim, I decided to apply for a Michigan death certificate for my grandfather...in the event he had died. Three weeks later came the envelope bearing the seal of the state of Michigan. Indeed, he had passed away. The certificate listed the funeral home and I called them. I was in for the shock of my life!

The funeral home agreed to send the obituary notice to me. I couldn't wait, and asked them to read it over the phone. My birth mother was alive, at least in 1971. My aunts were also listed as survivors.

Suddenly it stated Robert, Michael, Claudia, Sherry...grandchildren of my grandfather...children of Roberta...I had *brothers* and *sisters*!

It was a race back to the phone books, which had provided the answer before. Scouring all the phone books from cities the survivors were listed from, I almost came up empty.

An aunt from Tucson, Arizona, was listed. Tense feelings began in the pit of my stomach...should I call her? Would she remember anything? Would she tell me anything if she knew the answers? It took over a week to work up the courage to face what I might face and make the call.

Doris is the aunt that lives in Tucson. It was a Saturday night that I sat down to call her. She answered on the third ring (yes, I remember the details). "Hello?" I stumbled for words. Finally I asked her a bunch of "do you remember" questions. After letting me ramble questions...she asked very clearly, "Are you Roberta's missing son?"

I said, "Yes, I am Larry."

The tears began to flow...the spine is tingling as I write and recall this experience all these years later. "Yes, your mother is alive...you have brothers and sisters...your mother has been waiting for this phone call for over 36 years" were her next statements.

She then told me the story of my birth and my placement for adoption, not the reason for it. The tears overwhelmed me as I heard the story for the first time. I sat in stunned silence and let her speak and the tears flow.

After a long period, my next question, the important one: did she think my mother would want to talk to me?

"Yes," was the immediate reply. Doris wanted to be the one to break the news to my mother and asked for my phone number. She indicated it might be a few days before my mother called, as this would probably put her in total shock.

My partner and I went to dinner later that evening. When we arrived home, there was a message on our answering machine. "Larry, this is your mother. I will call back. I can't believe after all these years you have found me!" Needless to say, more tears followed.

I don't know how many times I listened to that message that night before we decided to go to bed. Less than a half hour after calling it a night, we were startled by the ringing phone. My partner answered the phone and could only say, "Larry, you want this call!"

That phone call will always remain private with me...it was and is the best phone call I have ever received. My mother and I spoke for almost four hours that first night. We talked about everything but why she gave me up...I wasn't ready to hear the answer. We ended the call by agreeing to write, do phone calls and hopefully someday meet. I wasn't ready to meet...it was *all* happening too fast for me.

The search had begun to find a family medical history and have a few questions answered. Now I faced: did I want to face the woman, no matter what the reason, who gave me up at birth? I did not know.

Chapter Eleven

FIRST LETTER TO BIRTH MOTHER

This is the letter I wrote for my birth mother shortly after I began my search for her in 1982. I would send it to her if I found her, whether she determined if she wanted contact with me or not. The next chapter tells you what happened to the letter.

Dear Mother,

It was a decision of a lifetime that with what was known and felt at the time was a proper decision. I will not judge you. I will never tell you what you did was wrong. It will never be my place to say. I was not mature or old enough to know the reasons why.

Never say you are sorry; never tell me that what you did so many years ago was wrong. I know in my heart that if you are like I know myself, it was what you thought was the right thing to do.

I will not confront you. I will make this as easy and safe for us both as possible. I just need to know that you are alive, what life has been for you since we parted. I may not have enough time to find you before you depart this life for a better one, but know that my prayers are with you.

I will defend you and your decisions in life as any son would. I will hold your memory true, even if all I know is your name. I will never defile your name, your circumstances or your decisions in life.

I know that I too have made many mistakes, but I have no regrets. Each mistake has made me a better person, turned me in a different direction, and made me care more for life than I ever would have before.

If you feel guilt, I will tell you that I feel that you should not harbor any. I have led a good and fulfilling life that I am proud of. Your decision has made my life today what it is. True, it would have been different, but I cannot say it would have been either better or worse. I am a product now of what I have lived and experienced.

To you, Mother, I pledge my gratitude for giving me all that I have. I have lost nothing now. I know who you are by name. The only thing I would ask in addition is to know you. I have many of your attributes. I hold every thought of you to be precious as gold.

I do not know what you look like; I do not know what you sound like. But to me, you are my guardian angel and have helped me through life without conscious awareness of you. I know you talk to me. You always have. You pray for my safety, happiness and well-being.

For the last 32 years, we have been connected. Sometimes I listened to you, sometimes I didn't. You are my "gut," my instinct, my heart and my thoughts.

Tonight I raise my glass in praise of your bravery, your life, and all the decisions you made.

Cheers to you, Mother. You did well.

Your son, Larry

Chapter Twelve

BIRTH MOTHER'S STORY

My birth mother and I continued to write and talk on the phone for a few months. Finally my partner and I decided it was time for us to meet.

I invited her from Pontiac, Michigan (only forty-five miles from where she lived when I was born), for an all-expense-paid trip to New York City, knowing she would not be able to afford the trip herself. I knew the meeting would be difficult for both of us, so I arranged a suite for her at a nearby hotel. This way, we both could spend some time alone to collect our thoughts and feelings. She accepted the invitation.

May 24, 1986, a day never to be forgotten by me. Newark International Airport. The day has arrived...36 years, 3 months, and 17 days after I was born...I would meet the woman who gave me life. To say I was tense or nervous would be putting it mildly. I arrived at the airport hours before the flight was due to arrive.

I brought with me 36 long- stemmed red roses, one for each year of life I had thus far been blessed with.

Should I call her mother? Should I hug her? What should I do? Let nature takes its course was the only answer that came back to me.

The plane taxis to the gate...there is no turning back now. There she was (I had an old photo of her that she had sent) walking down the ramp. We shook hands, then hugged. I called her Roberta, not Mother.

After getting her settled in her suite, we strolled down Fifth Avenue for a while. I took her to lunch and Central Park. As the day began turning to evening we went back to her hotel suite. It was time to hear the answer to the question that had yet to be asked or answered: why?

My father was her next-door neighbor. He had fought in World War II as a Merchant Marine and had returned to live with his folks. They had a date. I was conceived on that date! My father wanted nothing more to do with her. He had gotten what he was after.

My grandfather, being a strict Polish Roman Catholic, would not allow her to remain in the house and sent her off to a home for unwed mothers (Sarah Fisher Home) and told her "not to bring that bastard child home with her." She had three choices, either give birth and have no place to go...give me up for adoption and return home or have a back-alley abortion.

She gave birth in the early hours of February 7, 1950, and saw me only briefly before they took me away. She went home to go on with her life, but was never able to forget the baby she left behind, and hoped that one day I might look for her.

She hated her father for what he had forced her to do, and even though I learned he had been dead 15 years, the remaining hatred was still obvious.

She didn't realize that I was never adopted, but rather moved to various foster homes until eventually being sent to Boys Town. She thought I may have gone to Vietnam and been killed.

We both shed many tears that evening in her suite. I told her she made the only choice she could have made and was thankful she had not chosen abortion...for selfish reasons of course! We talked, cried, talked some more that first day deep into the night...we had over 36 years to relive!

My mother was born to John Robert Adams and Sarah Wray Adams on November 30, 1930, in Elmira, New York. She was the first of three daughters born to my maternal grandparents. In the height of the Depression my grandmother abandoned my grandfather, leaving him to raise three young girls on his own. My mother, being so young at the time, had no memories of her mother, not even her name. She never had a reason to request her birth certificate and would see her mother's name for the first time she could remember, when I presented it to her.

Her father struggled to make ends meet for a short while then decided to return to Michigan. He did not, however, return to his roots in Bay City, Michigan, but then made his home Detroit, Michigan.

Work was difficult for him to find and soon he realized he could not care for his daughters. He placed them in an orphanage so they would be provided for. They remained there until he married Alice in 1939. He and Alice did not have children together. She brought one son into the marriage, and the three girls soon joined them at home.

My mother never finished high school. At sixteen she went to work as a waitress at the downtown Hudson Department Store Restaurant.

After giving birth to me in 1950, she moved out of her family's home to try and make it on her own. She continued working as a waitress. To supplement her income, she did a photo shoot once in the nude. She never knew I was aware of this and had seen pictures of her.

In 1953, she married Robert Moore and moved to Florida. According to my mother it was not a good marriage and Robert was extremely abusive. My half-brothers were born and also as a result of a final abuse, one of my half-sisters was born. Mother left her husband and returned to Michigan to raise her four young children on her own. She divorced her husband and never remarried. She had worked all her life either as a waitress or at one of the automobile plants in the Detroit area. Sometimes, she worked both to make ends meet.

When we did meet, she stayed a week in NYC. I treated her to Broadway shows, and we toured all the sites of Manhattan and Liberty Island.

During that time, I learned other things. It became obvious very quickly she was an alcoholic. She told me of my youngest brother's drug addictions, my one sister's fancy for a different man each night, though she had two children. She also told me of the brother and sister who made it. In short, within the week she was in NYC I became even more thankful for her giving me up for adoption, for Boys Town and the life I have had.

A few months after our initial meeting, I took a trip to Pontiac, Michigan, to visit her and also meet my half-brothers and half-sisters for the first time. Two brothers and a sister, after meeting, told her they wanted nothing to do with me, as I wasn't their brother, but a stranger and it was best left that way. One sister (Claudia) did reach out and we had developed a warm, loving relationship over the years.

While on my visit there, my mother took out several photo albums to show me. She didn't realize how painful it would be for me to look at pictures of her past holidays, family events and the likes. Though I was thankful she gave me up, I did not want to see pictures I could have and should have been a part of.

Our relationship over the years following the initial meeting was strained at best. We had never developed a mother/son relationship. Of course, I had not expected that, since at 36 I did not need a mother to raise me. She remained an alcoholic in denial.

The relationship we had developed would be destroyed Christmas night 1998.

I had spent Christmas Eve with friends in Fargo, North Dakota, and got up very early the next morning for a 13-hour drive to Chicago, Illinois. My sister Claudia lives there with her family and my mother was visiting for the holidays. My sister thought it would be nice for us to spend one holiday together. I arrived in the evening weary and tired from the drive. They had waited Christmas dinner for my arrival.

Claudia, for some weird reason, has a television in her dining room and leaves it on during meals...even Christmas. During the meal a news story came on about gays/AIDS. I had never told my mother I was gay, as we did not have the close relationship I felt was needed to share that information. Claudia did know.

As the news story ended, my mother blurted out, "If I had a son that was gay I would wish he would get AIDS and die. I could not bear having a gay son!"

Claudia gasped and hollered, "MOM!"

My heart felt as though it had been broken and stomped upon a thousand times. I got up from the dinner table and quietly but clearly said, "You don't need to worry about a gay son, you just killed him." I walked out from my sister's home never to see my mother again.

When I left, I checked into a hotel, a 48-year-old man spending Christmas night crying myself to sleep. This is how my mother found out her first son is gay. My mother had "given me up" for a second time in my life. This time it was neither due to her strict father, or her inability to care for a child. Now it was simply because her son was gay. She not only gave me up...she wished I were dead!

Despite my mother's words, I hoped and prayed over the next three years that some degree of reconciliation between us would occur. She never attempted to call or write to say she was sorry for what she had said. I can only feel this is truly how she felt.

She suffered a stroke in 1999. Reconciliation did not happen between us and death took her suddenly in the fall of 2001. My mother died a very bitter and lonely woman.

I sent flowers with the card signed "Larry," and not "Son." I had made a promise to myself earlier that I would not attend the funeral and I did not attend the funeral. Though Claudia seemed to understand to a point why I chose to do what I did, it has destroyed our once close, loving relationship.

I got the answers to my medical questions. Heart problems do run in my mother's family. I also inherited her eye problems. She had a lazy left eye with 20/400 vision, as do I.

The answers to my questions about our heritage would have to be found on my own. My mother was not raised Polish. My grandfather hated his Polish heritage and changed his name completely in 1920 to join the US Marine Corps. That is why my name is not Piechowiak.

However, with her death I knew there was still some unfinished business that one day would have to be faced.

Over a year passed since my birth mother's death when I came to the full realization that her death left a gaping, bloody, festering, open wound deep within me.

Her death had denied us the opportunity of reconciliation, though there had been no evidence in the previous three years that this might happen.

Her death had denied me a final opportunity even to speak my mind to her as to how her words during our final meeting had been like a dagger to the heart.

I cannot say I wanted an opportunity to forgive. I felt then and feel now that my birth mother had committed the unforgivable. There was no reason for needing to forgive her for giving me up for adoption, for that had been a very wise and loving decision. However, how can one forgive another who after twelve years of a relationship wishes you dead only because you are gay? I cannot!

I, however, knew I needed to do something to allow this open wound to close and begin to heal. It will never completely heal but a scar can at least allow one to move on.

In an effort to reach out to my birth mother shortly after that devastating Christmas of 1998, I sent her a letter. It contained exactly how I felt from that experience. It contained the story of the struggle I had gone through, including attempted suicide, to accept myself for who I was. It contained my hope of a reconciliation between us. It did not ask that she approve of my being gay, rather just that she accept me as she had that day back in 1986…as her son, whether I was gay or not. That letter came back to me marked, "return to sender." I kept that letter through the final years of her life and in the time that had passed since her death.

This was only one of several attempts to reach out to my mother for a possible reconciliation. There were attempted phone calls…she only had to hear my voice and she would hang up.

Birthday and Christmas cards were sent by me those last three years only to have them also "returned to sender."

The most painful, brutal realities for me to deal with were the attempts by my half-sister to reach out to my mother on my behalf were also rejected. About a month before my mother's sudden passing, Claudia shared with me that she had again attempted to get my mother to either accept a call from me or make the call to me herself. My mother's words: "He's dead, leave it be!"

It appears though I was not physically dead, in my mother's eyes and heart I was in fact dead and would no longer be a part of her life.

A month later she herself was dead.

So the question after her death became: "How can I move on without forgiving?"

It took a few months of deeply emotional times contemplating this question. The answer would not come easy. It was an answer, however, that I knew I had to find for my own emotional well being and for healing to begin.

Suddenly the answer came clear out of the blue...you need to let it go! I knew right away how I hoped to accomplish this.

I very much enjoy biking. I have in my hometown discovered a place I enjoy going to: Eagle Point Park.

One early Saturday morning in June 2003, I set out for that place on my bike. I had with me the letter I had sent my birth mother four and a half years earlier.

Throughout the park are hideaways where one can light campfires. After biking awhile I found one spot that was hidden away more than others where I might have a needed time for privacy.

I built a small campfire. I took the letter and held it for a few minutes, then opened it. I slowly unfolded the pages as the emotions welled up inside me. I started to read the letter aloud...Dear Mother!

As I read each line, paragraph, or page the tears streamed more readily down my face, the voice cracked more often and the body trembled almost beyond control. I was determined to finish the letter, for I had to have my say. I continued on until the closing salutation..."the son you choose to give up a second time, Larry!"

When I had finished reading it I placed each page, one by one, upon the campfire and watched as the flames began to devour them.

As the smoke ascended to the heavens I verbalized the words, "I am now letting go."

I had read the words I had written my birth mother to her and was now sending them up to her to do as she wished. I had finally been able to say all that had been stored within my heart to her. I would no longer allow myself to be burdened with the baggage she had placed on me. *I was free!*

Yes, I could actually forgive my birth mother with that act even without totally realizing it at the time. This does not mean I will ever forget those wounds she had inflicted upon me. I, however, would no longer hold onto them. I gave her words as well as mine back to her. I had finally let go! I could move on! Everything was now in her court where it belonged. I had a few months earlier written to my half sister that had given up the relationship we had prior to our birth mother's death. It had been a last attempt to reach out to her just as I had done our mother. The letter did not come back but neither had she responded.

When I felt comfortable with everything involving my mother I took a blank sheet of paper to symbolize the last letter to my half-sister and placed it also on the fire. I was also letting go of her as well.

I continued to watch as each page turned from paper to ashes.

When it was obvious that there was no more to burn, I doused the fire with the water bottle I had brought with me. I then gathered up the wet ashes and carried them to a secluded spot amongst the trees. I dug a small hole and placed the ashes with it. I then covered them with the dirt and some brush found nearby. I had not attended my mother's funeral but on this day I had my own private one. I buried not only ashes of my letter but also all the pain and anguish caused by her and in doing so I believe I also buried my mother.

I slowly walked away from that spot. I could feel the gaping wound was already beginning to get just a bit smaller. The healing has begun.

I remember her in prayer. I pray that in death she has found the peace that she was unable or unwilling to obtain in life. I also still thank her for giving me the opportunity of life.

Rest in peace, Mother, I forgive you!

My birth mother and me at Southport Pier in Manhattan with Brooklyn Bridge in the background, taken May 25, 1986.

Chapter Thirteen

A FINAL LETTER TO BIRTH MOTHER

This is the letter I wrote my birth mother after the collapse of our relationship on Christmas Day 1998. As you already know, she never read the letter. I, however, shared it with her in June 2003 when the original letter was read to her then burned. Sharing this letter now is my final act of letting go of the pain and anguish her actions caused me and moving on with my life.

December 28, 1998

Dear Mother,

This is a very difficult letter for me to write as tears are still in my eyes for my heart is broken.

I never thought I would hear with my own ears the words you expressed on Christmas Day.

I know our relationship in the twelve years since we reunited has not always been a good one. In honesty, I know at times it has been quite strained.

Despite this strain I believe we both have some much cherished memories as well.

I thought this being our very first Christmas together, would provide yet another of those cherished memories...instead my heart was broken.

I have known pain in my life, but I don't think I have ever felt the pain I now feel. There I was on Christmas night, in a hotel room alone, crying myself to sleep. The pain has not lessened in the few days that have followed.

Sixteen years ago I began a search for you. It was a long, trying and at times painful search...but it ended in success.

I had another long, trying, painful search in my life. The search for and acceptance of myself.

I began questioning my sexuality at a young age. However, I knew what was going through my head went contrary to everything I had ever been taught. I did not want to be what I thought I was. I fought it every way I possibly could. I went with girls thinking that it would cure me of my thoughts...it did not. I went to counseling in hopes it could steer me straight...it did not. I even went to a priest friend for help...all he did was condemn me to hell.

The thought that I could be gay tormented me throughout my high school years into college. I tried to find solace in a bottle. This only temporarily released me of the pain.

The anguish became so tortuously painful for me that I thought there was only one way for me to end it...that was to end my own life.

I tried and failed. Failing, however, gave me the opportunity to meet a wonderful counselor. She made me realize that through all these years of pain and torment I was only denying who I was. I was not choosing to be gay...I was born gay. I should accept and be proud of the person I was. She said many other things in the times we shared together but this was the beginning of the healing I had so long searched.

Yes, Mother, I am gay. No, I did not choose to be gay. Who in their right mind would make such a choice? It's a choice that could cause a life of possible verbal or physical assault, loss of friends or even loss of family.

I have already suffered three of the four, now I face the possibility of the fourth.

I am who I am, Mother. I cannot be anything but who I am.

However, I am still the same person I was just moments before you uttered your hateful words. I am still the son you gave birth to...only now you are aware of one more part of my being.

Being gay does not make me any less loving a son than I have been. It doesn't make me any less the person you were once proud of.

I know this has come as a shock to you. I don't expect you to understand it nor even condone it. I only hope that you can accept it and accept me, not as your gay son but as your son that happens to be gay.

I have accepted you, your good points as well as those I do not agree with...I only ask the same in return.

Many years ago you were faced with a decision. I know how painful that decision was for you. The decision you made was due to the circumstances you found yourself in of which you were not in control. You made the decision to give me away for adoption. It was a decision that you thought was best for me. You would not know what that decision caused me in the years that would follow. However, I have never held that decision against you.

You now face that decision once again. This time you are in total control of the decision you make.

Are you going to give me up as your son a second time? This is your decision and yours alone.

This time you need to do the searching. You need to search within yourself and decide can you or can you not accept and live with the fact that your first born son is gay.

I know what you said on Christmas Day. I can only hope and pray that it was not what you truly meant. Do you really wish I would get AIDS and die? Would you really be happier to have a dead son rather than a son that is gay?

We have overcome many obstacles during the past twelve years. It had not been an easy road for either of us at times. We are both stubborn and hard headed at times...but hey, those are traits I inherited from you. This obstacle too can be overcome...but it is your decision!

I can forgive if you can accept. I don't believe that is asking too much from either of us.

We missed so much in the years we were apart. No matter how hard we try we cannot make up for those years. We were, however, given a second chance. A chance to experience things I thought would never be possible. I don't know how many years we may have to continue our second chance...are you willing to throw whatever those years are away?

We have missed so much together already, I would hate for us to miss so much more.

I cannot force you to decide anything. It is your decision to make. Again, I can only hope and pray it will be a decision that will allow us to spend more time together.

I don't know, as I write this, if you will in fact read it to its conclusion. I don't know if you do in fact read it, you will end up crumbling it up and discarding it without giving me a reply.

Whether you reply or not, whether you in fact already consider me dead...I want you to know the following:

I remain glad I took the time and effort to find you. I am glad we were able to be reunited. I am glad we had an opportunity to have some cherished memories. I am glad I have been able to call myself your son.

No matter your decision, I will always be your son. Your decision will only determine if in your heart and mind if I am a son alive or am I dead.

I await your decision.

Your son you may choose to give up a second time,
Larry

Chapter Fourteen

BIRTH FATHER'S STORY

I did not begin a search for my birth father until I had found my birth mother. I purposely chose not to do so until then. Though I had his name, I felt I had enough on my plate just searching for my birth mother.

During the initial meeting with my mother, I had asked her about my father. Other than telling me that he was the next-door neighbor and agreeing the name I had was correct, she provided no information. I would have to attempt to find him by myself.

It was back to the NYC Library once again to scour the phone books for Detroit from 1950 through 1986. There was not a single Robert Irwin Marx listed, nor was it listed in any other variation.

During my earlier search, I had learned many things about searching for someone. Thus, with the above result, I did not feel like I was at a dead end. I tried various other resources but each produced the same negative result.

I was down to my last avenue and I thought it would be a just shot in the dark. I had earlier checked the Polk City Directory for 1950. I had found my grandfather's listing, but did not see a Marx listing. The listing given for my grandfather's neighbor was a Clarence/Ruth Weikert. However, if I was to believe my mother, my father was her next-door neighbor.

I decided to write to the Wayne County Board of Elections, my last resource, to see if my father had registered to vote. I gave the neighbor's address as his.

Three weeks later, an envelope came from the Wayne County Elections Board. Bingo…I had hit pay dirt! There was my father's name, date of birth and address, as I had submitted it, and his mother's maiden name: Ruth Goode. Ruth had obviously married Clarence Weikert. The question arose as to why was my father's father named Marx? I didn't waste too much time on that question at the moment, as I figured if I found my father I would get an answer then.

I remembered the company listing for Clarence Weikert in the Polk Directory. I checked with the Detroit phone book for 1990 (four years had passed since this search began) to see if the company was still listed. It was!

A simple deduction by me concluded that Clarence had long since retired from the company, but maybe they could provide me with a little information. I took time to make up a story for my calling and placed the call. Yes, Clarence had retired and according to their records was deceased. They could give me the phone number of his daughter that was listed on their records as the person to contact in the event of an emergency. I gladly took the phone number.

I took a few days to sort through my thoughts and approach before making the call. I remembered the awkwardness of my call to my birth mother's sister four years earlier.

Finally the call was made. I babbled some story about doing genealogical research, a partial truth. After asking Judy several general questions about family, I asked her about her brother Robert. Why was his last name Weikert and not Marx?

She indicated that her mother remarried after Robert's father ran off when he was a child. After confirming that information, I determined it was time to tell Judy the truth.

I simply said, "I was looking for Robert in particular."

Her reply, "Oh my God! Are you who I think you are?"

"If you think I am Robert's son, the answer is yes," I said.

She repeated, "Oh my God!"

After we got a few more oh my Gods out of the way, we began an hour conversation. She asked my name. I asked how she knew about me and did my father know? She said it was family conversation many years ago and that yes, my father did know about me. Judy was close to my mother's age when I was born, she remembered my mother going away in late 1949. Her mother told her it was because she was pregnant and that her brother was the father.

The Weikerts and my grandparents, being neighbors, were close and shared family information. My paternal step-grandmother also shared with them when I was born, my name and that I was being placed for adoption.

I continued general conversation, asking questions about my father and then came the key question. "Would my father acknowledge my existence and would he talk with me?"

She felt that he would not deny I was his son, but could not answer if he would talk with me or not. She and my father had not communicated with each other for a couple years, due to a family quarrel. She felt the best thing for me was to call my father directly and proceeded to give me his phone number since it was unlisted. She also gave me his address in case I decided to write him instead.

I made the decision that I would not wait for the mail, but would call him. After working up the courage for a few hours, I placed the call. It seemed the phone rang forever. Finally a woman's voice answered. I asked if I could speak to Robert and was told to hang on. The heart raced and hands trembled as I waited.

Suddenly I heard, "Hello." It was my father.

I responded with, "Hello, is this Robert?"

"Yes," was the reply.

I made an instinctive decision to not beat around the bush. "Robert, if you're not sitting down I suggest you do so for what I am about to tell you," I said.

"I'm okay, go ahead," he said.

"Robert, this is your son Larry calling," I blurted out.

The silence was deafening. "Robert, did you hear me?" I said after waiting a few moments.

"Yes, how did you find me?" was his reply. Without saying it directly, he was acknowledging I was his son!

I needed to hear directly from him that I was his son! "You know you have a son named Larry?" I asked.

"Yes, I do. Did my sister Judy help you find me?" he answered. He seemed more concerned about how I found him, rather than the fact that I did find him and it was his son talking with him for the first time in forty years.

I told him of the search for Roberta, my birth mother, which had concluded fours years earlier. He asked a few general questions about her. I then told him of the past four years of searching for him and how it had all fallen into place just a few days earlier.

He seemed shocked by what I was able to do. He asked a few questions about me. It did not turn out to be the type of first conversation I had with my birth mother. It seemed somewhat distant and cold. I chalked it up to the suddenness of this being presented to him. I felt we might just need some time.

We agreed to communicate further through letters and maybe one day plan on meeting. With that, a thirty-minute or so conversation was over. I did not have the elated feeling I did when I hung up from my birth mother for that first time. I felt somewhat numb and out in the cold.

We did keep our commitment to write each other. He wrote his first letter to me a few days after our conversation. Though more feelings were expressed in it, it still seemed to be rather general in nature. I do still have his first letter, though it is beginning to fade with age.

My father was born in Detroit, Michigan, in 1924. He never knew his birth father, as he ran out when he was but a baby. His mother was Ruth (Goode) Marx. She had remarried and thus, the Weikert name came into the family.

My father was not the best of communicators. Due to WWII, he joined the Merchant Marines and was shipped overseas in the midst of his junior year of high school. After the war he came home and lived with his parents, my mother's next-door neighbors.

My father told a somewhat different story than my mother of what happened between them. I imagine it is somewhere in between. I repeat each of their stories and let them stand as told.

He and my mother dated during the winter of 1948-1949. He remembers during the spring, around May, her coming to him and telling him she was pregnant. He said he offered to marry her, to make things right, and she refused. He remembers her father sending her away during the summer of 1949.

By the time she gave birth to me, placed me for adoption and came home, he had moved. He never saw her again nor did he ever see me. His mother told him of my birth, my name and that my mother left me at the hospital to be placed for adoption. He was honest with me in saying that once he learned of this, he put her and me out of his mind and went on with his life.

In 1952, he married his first wife Pauline. It was a bitter marriage, which ended in 1955. It was a marriage, however, that produced a half sister for me, Susan.

He remarried in 1957 to Angie. Angie was roughly ten years older than him and brought her four children into the marriage. My father and Angie never had children together.

My half-sister Susan spent her growing-up years after the divorce with her mother Pauline. She rarely saw our father. However, when she was married, she did ask him to walk her down the aisle. Susan and I exchanged one letter. She wrote first and I answered. I never got a reply to that letter and I have not heard from her in the years that have followed.

My father worked for the Michigan Central Railroad his entire working career. He was forced to retire in 1978 due to a severe heart attack. In 1987, he underwent triple bypass surgery.

My father and I met one time. In the spring of 1992, I was on a business trip to Detroit and called him. I asked if we could finally meet. He was hesitant, but finally agreed and gave me directions to his home in Taylor, Michigan.

He greeted me at the gate and we went around to the back patio. He introduced me to Angie, who then went into the house. I can't honestly say I have any feeling about the meeting. He appeared cold and distant as he had since I found him. The fact that I was there in person didn't seem to cause any change in him. I stayed only an hour, as I did not feel comfortable. During the time there, I was not invited into his home nor offered any beverage or anything.

At least I could say I met the man who, because of sperm, was my father. He did not fill the role of father or even friend in the way most would understand the terms.

After my meeting with him, our letters became less frequent. Part of it I know was due to the cataracts he had in both eyes, making reading and writing difficult. I also believe it was partially due to his wanting to keep a distance between us.

My father had cataract surgery performed in April of 1994. On July 24, 1994, he suffered a heart attack and died. Though I sent condolences to his sister Judy, I did not feel the need to attend his funeral. Aunt Judy and I have maintained erratic communication in the years that have followed. She is the only one on my father's side of the family to do so. I have never met her or any other member of my father's family. Angie, his wife, died just three months after my father in October 1994.

I learned through Aunt Judy, after my father's death, that my mother was *not* the first woman he got pregnant and abandoned. He also got a German girl pregnant in 1944. She had a son and my father abandoned her after she gave birth. I discovered she committed suicide in 1946. Her son, another brother, is not to be found.

Judy also gives my mother's story about my birth more credence than my father's, but this might be due to the problems between them during the last six years of his life.

It is amazing how history has repeated itself in my family. My birth father came from a broken home. His father had deserted his mother when he was a young boy. His mother later divorced his father and remarried...he had no memory of his birth father.

My birth mother also came from a broken home. Her mother deserted her father shortly after her youngest sister was born. My mother had no recollections of her mother.

Despite what both my birth parents faced as youths themselves, they repeated the same destructive cycle. How unfortunate for them and for us kids that they brought into the world.

I am a far way from completing my journey into my past. Finding my birth mother and finding out my heritage on her side is Polish has opened a whole new world of discovery for me. I have to be honest and say I have not had the same interest to do a genealogical search on my birth father's side of the family. With him I now know my full heritage is Polish/German. This new world of discovery goes on now as it has in the past ...but *wow*, what results I have found.

In closing the story about my search and finding my birth parents, I must say that despite how things have turned out with my immediate family, I *do not* regret making the decision to search for them. I was not looking for a "family relationship." Until I found them, I had no family to call my own and survived. I could continue to survive with little or no family...there would not be a difference from the past.

I now know who I am and where I came from. My heritage has been opened up to me. For the first time in my life, I have some sense of belonging, no matter how my family reacted to me. They couldn't kill the feelings I had inside. I believe the search and the results just made me an even stronger person. I am happy I did the search and now even knowing what I know, I would repeat it. I have no regrets!

My birth father taken the year of my birth: 1950.

Chapter Fifteen

FIRST CHRISTMAS

It seems strange for a man of my age to be speaking of "first Christmas." However, Christmas 2002 was exactly that for me.

I had attempted to spend a first Christmas with my birth mother and sister in 1998. It turned into a disaster. My birth mother, that Christmas night, wished I had AIDS and was dead because I am gay.

Prior to that experience, I had never had the opportunity to celebrate Christmas with any member of my "real family." I went through my youth and most of my adult life not even knowing I had a family I could call my own. If you have read the chapters prior to this, you know that began to change in 1986 as I found my birth mother. It took 12 years before I considered spending a Christmas with her, a decision I have since regretted.

After the experience of Christmas 1998, I swore I would never again attempt to spend a Christmas with family if the opportunity arose, which I did not expect to happen. I had gone 48 Christmases without a family to call my own and spend the holidays with, I could go through the rest of my life in the same way.

2001 and 2002 were years of discovery and brought many extended family members into my life. I had found and met my cousins Dorothy, Roger, David and wife Ann, and Carol. It was a time of discovery and joy I had not experienced before. I had met my cousin Carol (Luczak side of the family) during a visit to Michigan in September. She issued an open invitation for me to spend Thanksgiving and Christmas with her and her family. Since I was relocating due to a new job at the time, Thanksgiving was not possible. However, I would be in the Chicago area for Christmas and could have a few days off during the holidays if I wanted. I gave her invitation serious consideration. The wound of 1998 still had not healed, thus I was apprehensive and hesitant to accept the invitation. In the end, I accepted, thinking it could never be as bad as 1998. I would go to Carol's house from December 20th-25th. I would have to return to Chicago late Christmas Day so I could work that night. Thus, begins my story of "First Christmas."

I worked through the night of December 19th and early morning hours of the 20th. I then began the five-hour drive to Midland, Michigan, where Carol lives. The hesitancy and apprehension I had immediately melted away as I was greeted at the door with a huge, long bear hug by Carol. The holiday was at least off to a good start.

Despite my being exhausted, Carol and I sat at her kitchen table talking and filling ourselves with coffee. After a dinner of homemade chicken soup, we moved to the living room to watch a little TV. As I made myself comfortable on the couch, I knew I was not long before falling asleep. I wasn't, and soon I was dead to the world. Carol shared with me the next morning that I lay there with my arms across my chest and she thought of going to get a rose to place in them as she knew I was definitely done for that night.

The next day, after taking awhile to get ourselves in gear, we decided to go over to Frankenmuth, Michigan. Frankenmuth is an old German community and also home to Bronner's. Bronner's is a year-round Christmas store with thousands of square feet of display, for anything you could ever imagine wanting for Christmas. People travel there from around the world. I would make sure to keep my credit cards in my pocket! Bronner's also does enormous Christmas displays outside year round. We were there during the day, thus didn't see it lit up but could tell it would have been magnificent. After strolling through the store we made a visit to their "Silent Night Chapel" and then to the Bavarian Inn Restaurant for lunch.

That evening, we attended mass at the local parish, St. Anthony's, and then met friends of Carol (Jerry and Deborah) for dinner. It had been yet another full day, a good day, and I was ready for sleep.

Sunday, Carol got the best of me twice in one day. While we were just out and about during the afternoon she indicated we needed to go to a fabric store to pick out material for a gift her daughter Dee was making. She wanted me to go in the store with her to give my opinion. I should have known better! She was looking for a bear pattern for the front of a blanket with a solid pattern for the reverse side. I ended up picking the fabric, the pattern and the color; boy, was she willing to have me do it. Christmas Day I would find out why.

Carol was running behind on her gift wrapping. Figuring there couldn't be that many, I opened my mouth and volunteered to help. Once I started they just kept coming out…more, more and more until I thought it wouldn't end.

She got me twice in one day but I enjoyed every minute of it!

Monday, Carol and I had set aside for a trip into Bay City, Michigan. We both had some research we wanted to do, as well as make a couple of visits. It turned out to be a special day in more ways than one.

We started out at the Bay County Courthouse to do some tracking on my great grandfather's homestead. We were able to find various records, except for when the two-lot property was actually divided.

Since it would be the only day I would be in Bay City, we had to go to Krzysiak's, a local Polish restaurant, for lunch. It was worth the trip!

I had met my cousin Dorothy earlier in 2002. I decided I wanted to make a surprise visit to her to wish her Happy Holidays. While at Krzysiak's I picked up a box of "Chrusciki," a Polish pastry, to take her.

I must say I definitely surprised her, but she had a surprise of her own in store for me. She had me go into her bedroom to get a box she had planned on sending me after the holiday rush. Inside was a handmade afghan she had made just for me. It was beautiful. I consider it a family heirloom and something I will treasure for years to come.

Dorothy recently turned 89 years old. Though she is limited in her movements due to health problems she is still alert as can be. It is a delight when I have a chance to spend time with her. It was one of the memorable events of the holiday weekend. After an hour or so, it was time to move on.

We proceeded on to St. Stan's Cemetery. Both Carol and I had visits we wanted to make. I wanted to make a stop at the grave of my great grandparents. I am sure it had been many years since someone last paid their respects during the holiday time.

Another highlight of the day now was about to happen. I had been by the family homestead every time I had visited Bay City, but had never worked up the courage to go to the door and knock to see if the current owners might let me in to view the house from the inside. Carol had done this in November and said a few things about it; however, it's not like doing it oneself.

The outside of the home has changed significantly over the 112 years since it was built. There used to be four entrances into the house, one on each side. Now there are just two. The wraparound porch has been removed for a separate small front porch and a back porch. However, the inside has seen little change. I walked into the living room where my great grandparents, their children and many relatives had gathered so many times. To the left of the front door was the bedroom of my great grandparents. As one preceded you entered the dining room, off to the right of the dining room was the bedroom where the two girls of the family slept. To the left of the dining room you walked into the kitchen. I could picture the huge round table in the kitchen that my cousin Dorothy had described. I also could see the old stairway leading up to the second floor. Here eleven uncles had once slept dormitory style. The upstairs has now been divided into two rooms. The stairway to the upstairs by the kitchen had been closed and a new one made off the living room. I could picture where the stairway was Dorothy had described, leading to my great grandmother's special closet and also down to the fruit cellar. I did not take pictures of the inside of the house as it would have intruded on the privacy of the current owner and I was just grateful he had allowed me to walk through the house. One can only imagine the thoughts and pictures going through my mind as I walked through the house…unbelievable, awesome!

The day came to a delightful close as we spent time visiting friends of Carol's, Bob and Pat Fenton.

Christmas Eve 2002 began as any normal day would except it was so peaceful out in the countryside of Midland, Michigan. We would be going to a Midnight Mass, though celebrated at 5:00 p.m. Few parishes celebrate actual Midnight Mass anymore. We would then gather at Deborah and Jerry's for food, drink and merriment.

Before the celebrating could begin, it was realized that despite all my earlier wrapping efforts, Carol was still far behind in having gifts ready with Christmas just hours away. Again, I volunteered myself, and again Carol just kept bringing out more, more and more. Each member of Carol's family gets their individual Christmas stocking and each thing had to be individually wrapped. Carol now of course is in wrapping debtor's prison with a lengthy sentence to endure.

By 3:00 p.m. it was rush time to get ready to be at church early so we might participate in caroling before mass. We made it in the nick of time. Towards the end of the carol program three Christmas songs were chosen to have one verse sung in English followed by another in Polish. It was the first time I ever had heard Christmas carols sung in the native language of my great grandparents. It was a moving experience for me as were other parts of the mass as it progressed.

Mass ended around 7:00 p.m. and we drove to Deborah and Jerry's. As we drove we mentioned that it didn't appear it would be a white Christmas as no snow was on the ground. A disappointment, but for me a small one, as this was turning out to be a Christmas for me to remember.

The house was full of people throughout the evening. A wide variety of foods presented themselves, including some traditional Polish dishes. At one point all of us gathered in the living room for an exchange of gifts. Deborah even saw to it that there was one under the tree for me.

Shortly after midnight we gathered our things to head home, as within a few hours it would be the beginning of a long day.

Merry Christmas 2002! The morning dawned early for me. After getting the coffee pot going I looked out the window and what a surprise! It was a white Christmas after all. It had snowed in the few hours I had been asleep. The dream of a "white Christmas" had come true and just added another layer of memories.

Carol awoke not long after I did. To be honest, I banged on her door to wake her. :) Soon the house would be filled with her children as well as their children. We had the chance to spend some quality time talking before we were overrun.

Carol's family has a tradition for Christmas. They gather for a Christmas brunch, open presents then go to other families for visits. The breakfast consists of potato pancakes, Polish sausage, meatballs, eggs and toast. I got volunteered again this morning as a hungry mob filled the house and brunch was not quite ready.

Brunch was over and all gathered in the living room for the excitement of trashing wrapping paper throughout. I received some very, very precious gifts that day. Ali and Marissa, my nieces, besides each buying a small gift, made special signs for me. They are framed and hang on my bedroom wall today!

If you remember Sunday of the weekend I told you about buying fabric. I found out as I opened a box that I didn't just pick a fabric, but picked fabric for my own gift...they got me! Inside was a tied blanket with bears on one side and a solid blue with bear imprints on the other, which Dee had spent hours making in the few days since the fabric was bought. There were other gifts, though I asked Carol not to do so, but those two are the most memorable.

It was fast approaching 3:00 p.m., time I must depart for the five-hour drive back to Chicago for work that night.

I had throughout the weekend had many emotional moments of this cherished holiday, which I had been able to keep private behind the closed door of my bedroom. However, as I began gathering things to take to my truck I passed Carol, as I leaned down to give her a bear hug and a thank you for a Christmas I would not forget, the tears began to flow for us both.

Four years earlier I had cried myself to sleep in pain because of the rejection of my birth mother for a second time. Now I cried in joy for the beautiful memories I would cherish.

A fast departure would have to be made, but I had miles to reflect on this Christmas and admit having to pull alongside the road a few times. What can I say about Christmas 2002, my first Christmas? I had spent 52 years of life waiting for this one Christmas, which I thought I would never have. I cherished only one Christmas of the past. I had exchanged lifetime bonds with a fellow classmate at Boys Town 34 years before. Now after a lifetime, including 20 years of genealogical research, I actually had "real" family of my own to celebrate Christmas with.

Though I received many gifts this Christmas the greatest gift I will cherish throughout the rest of my life is the openness, the love and the memories given me by Carol and *all* her family. I came "home" for Christmas this year. If I am never able to again…this first Christmas will never be forgotten.

First cousin Dorothy and I in 2003, months from her 90th birthday.

Second cousin Carol and I on Christmas Eve 2002 in Bay City, Michigan, at Jerry and Deborah's home.

My "first Christmas" family gathers for a photo-op: Gregory, Busia, Rick, me, Tracy, Carol, Liane, Madison, Marissa and Ali. Dee is not in the picture; she was taking it.

Chapter Sixteen

WHY DID I SEARCH?

I originally told my story on a website created for the Internet in early 1998. In it, I had one page that dealt with the search for my birth mother. The page generated numerous e-mails and guest book signings asking me questions. Why search? Why not leave the past alone? What do you hope to gain from your search? These were just a few of the questions asked.

Most questions came from people who were raised by their birth parents. They knew their heritage. They had extended family with whom to share their lives. They knew of potential medical problems that might arise in their lives.

They had no understanding or appreciation for those of us who have gone through life without any of the above or the void it left within us. They do not know what it would be like not to have any of the above.

I think now is a good time to answer the questions.

Through the first thirty-two years of my life I did not care about birth parents, family, heritage or any of that stuff. I had enough issues involved in just growing up and making something of myself, without having to spend time contemplating that bigger picture.

If you have read the pages prior to this one, you know that when I suffered my first heart attack in 1981, I was embarrassed when I could not answer the doctor's questions about "my family medical history." I had to answer, "I don't know." Despite this event, I let it pass and went on with dealing with the everyday issues of life.

The possibility of the issue arising again occurred a year later, when I applied for my first passport to travel to Greece.

I should note, to this point of my life, I did not know even the names of my birth parents. I had no interest in knowing them or anything about them partly due to a story told to me by foster parents around the age of seven.

Seven-year-olds can be quite inquisitive. I was no exception. I asked my foster parents, the Monshors, "Why couldn't I be with my mom and dad? Why was I kept moving from home to home?" Difficult questions for an adult to answer, even more difficult for a seven-year-old to have to ask or deal with.

Their answer probably shaped my attitude towards my birth mother for years to come. It was, "Your mother did not want you and threw you away in a trash can outside the hospital where you were born when you were two days old. A sister from the hospital found you. You were near death when she found you (remember, it was dead of winter…February). The good sisters named you. The court is trying to find a loving family to take you in as their son, but hasn't found the right one yet."

I don't know if the answer they gave at the time, which I know now was not true, was given because they were trying to protect me, or if they were trying to help me face the harsh reality of my circumstances. Perhaps they hoped by telling me this story, it would preclude my ever wanting to find my birth mother.

I know at the time, it was like a dagger in the heart. I was stunned and dumbfounded as to why someone who gave birth to me wouldn't want me as their son. I hated my birth mother! I thought I would never want anything to do with her. I placed this answer and pain deep within my memory and heart.

I did not raise the issue again for the next twenty-five years. By the time I did, the Monshors were both deceased.

I received my birth certificate from the state of Michigan so I could get my passport. There, for the first time, I saw the name of my birth mother: Roberta Adams. I also saw the address of her home at the time of my birth. No father was listed. The pain and hatred stored deep within me for so many years came bubbling to the surface. Despite this, I knew I somehow wanted questions answered.

My search went far beyond even my wildest dreams. You see the results within this book. The question still is: why? Why did I go beyond the original intent of getting simple medical information? Why did I want to find my birth mother? Why did I ever want to meet her? Why did I want to know my roots? Why take twenty years spending great amounts of time, energy and money researching my family history? Why look for living members of an extended family?

Every child, at some point, questions who they are, where they came from and so forth. Most are able to have the answers easily provided by a parent or other member of their family. Adoptees or many children of the foster care system, such as I, do not have that available to them. For adoptees in particular, of my generation, it is denied them by law. We are expected to go through life never knowing the answers to those questions. Many are even ridiculed for entertaining such questions.

I searched for the answers to all those questions because I am like any other normal individual. More importantly, I had the right to know! I searched first for information, then to fill a void in my life. I would like to think if the search had ended with just information, I would have been satisfied. Of course, knowing all I do today, it might not have been. Each person searching needs to know when enough is enough for them.

My search had its ups and downs. My initial search to just find the information needed to locate my birth mother to get medical information took four years. It would take another four years before I would find and meet my birth father. They have both since passed away. During that time, I learned how to be a detective, to ask questions that to most would have appeared stupid. I even had to learn to lie to just get the information I wanted.

Attempting to find my birth mother only aroused more questions within me. It was during the search, receiving my grandfather's death certificate, that I learned I was Polish. My mother's maiden name should have been Piechowiak. It became Adams only because of my grandfather, being ashamed of his heritage, changing his name. I now knew I had a heritage. I wanted to find out more. I decided I would do a genealogical search, whether I had ever found my birth mother or not. Each step of my search answered some questions, but also raised many new ones.

I found my birth mother, my birth father, as well as siblings. None were very cooperative in answering my questions about family health, heritage or genealogy. If they had been, it might have saved me sixteen more years of research.

I have found most of the answers to my questions. The void that was in my life has been filled. I now feel I am a whole person; I know who I am and where I came from. I am now in the position that children raised by their birth parents are in. I no longer have to feel different or abnormal. I found far more information about my family genealogy than I ever expected to. I found and met members of my extended family. I can now see in pictures family resemblances and say…see, I belong! In learning about my great grandparents, aunts, uncles and Polish people as a whole, I learned, in so many ways, why I am the person I am today.

This is why I and others search. We have the desire to be made whole. The desire to know that even when your birth parents may reject you, you still are a part of a family and a heritage. I had a good life prior to beginning my search and have done well during the search. The end result of my search just has made it better.

My initial search was, in comparison to adoptees', relatively easy despite the length of time it took. I know adoptees who have been searching for years, without success, to find the very basic of information: a birth parent name. This is due to he laws concerning adoption still on the books in many states.

Since the 1970s, some states have opened up their adoption laws, opening adoption registries. Many adoption agencies now enter into open-adoption agreements. However, in many cases, the adoptee is at a distinct disadvantage if they choose to search for their birth parents or any information that might identify who they are.

Though things have improved in the past twenty or so years, much more needs to be done. Most state adoption registries require both the birth parent and the adoptee grant permission for identifying information to be shared with the other party. If consent is not given or if nothing is on file indicating either way, any requests for information will be denied.

Current laws, even with updates, still play havoc for those adoptees from the 1930s, 1940s and even 1950s. In many cases, the birth parents or adoptee do not know the new laws regarding adoption registries. Also, the birth parents or now adult adoptees have passed away. Even in death, information cannot be given.

In most cases, the law that supposedly was "in the best interest of the child" has become "best interest of the birth parent, dead or alive."

I firmly believe *all* have the right to know who they are, where they came from, family heritage and genealogy, no matter the circumstances under which they came into this world.

To those who are not adoptees, or from a situation such as mine, I ask you, "Knowing all that you know today about yourself, family, family history, how would you have liked to have all that information kept from you? Would it leave a void in your life?" These are the conditions under which adoptees are expected to live. In truth, you know you would not like to live this way; why would you expect an adoptee to be any different from you?

I have known adoptees, even when the release of medical information about family could have saved their lives, were refused their request for information. This is wrong and has absolutely no justification. Why, when millions around the world who were raised by their birth parents do genealogical research to learn more about themselves and their heritage, is it considered normal? When an adoptee or person in my situation does the same it's considered abnormal? Seems hypocritical to me!

To birth parents, I have a message. We understand, in most cases, your decision to give up your child was made only after a great struggle within yourself. We know what a painstaking decision it was that you made. We know you made that decision because of the love you had for your child, and that you wanted what was best for him or her. I ask that you continue to act in the best interest of your child, who is now an adult and no matter how good a home they went to, or how well they have done in life, may still feel incomplete. *Please*, file information with your respective state adoption agency from which your child was adopted. Give your consent to have it released to your child when they reach adulthood. Let them fill the void within their lives. Without your consent this information will never be made known to them.

Adult adoptees, your birth parents also may be in the same position as you are. They may want to see how your life has turned out. To know they did indeed make the best decision for you that they could. You could do your part as well, provide updated information to the same agency mentioned above and give consent to have it released to a birth parent or sibling if requested. This is a two-way street, not a one-way.

Adult adoptees, who search for answers, do not mean you any harm. They do not want to disrupt the lives you have since built for yourselves. They just want and need answers to questions to which only you can unlock the door. Even if you do not wish for any type of relationship with your child, provide the information that would allow them to be whole.

My search was satisfied when I was able to sit with my birth mother and find out the true story of my birth; the gut-wrenching decision she made to give me up, and why; my true Polish heritage and the vague medical history that would allow me to better care for myself. I would have been satisfied if she had just provided me these facts in a letter and not agreed to meet me. I would have had the basic information I desired.

The fact she agreed to meet me, despite how our relationship turned out, was above and beyond what I had hoped for or expected during my search. Of course, because I found out I was Polish and because my grandfather was ashamed of this heritage, I continued my research to find out as much as I possibly could about my family.

I wanted to know why and when my ancestors came to America, what they did with their lives...I wanted to be proud of them. I have achieved that goal.

My only real regret is that I waited so long before I began to search. If I had begun at age eighteen or twenty-one, I might have been able to meet many aunts and uncles who were still living at the time. By the time I did begin my search and found all eleven children of my great grandparents, they were deceased. What a missed opportunity on my part.

I have been privileged to get to know some of my extended family and they have added so much to the picture. Through them, pictures and stories have been shared with me. You can only imagine the intense feelings I had when I saw the pictures of my birth parents, great grandparents or other family members for the first time; the feelings when I walked through the homestead my great grandfather built with his own hands 112 years ago; the feelings when sitting with an 89-year-old first cousin and hearing stories of my great grandparents, her mother, aunts and uncles or the feelings when being able, at the age of 52, to spend my first Christmas with family I could call my own. Many of the feelings, stories and now memories have been shared in other parts of this book.

Twenty years ago, I knew nothing of my birth mother, my heritage or my family history. Today, I know more than I had ever expected to be able to know. Even though I feel I have had a successful life to this point, it is only today that I can declare...I am whole! I finally have a sense of belonging, of knowing who I am. I am finally proud of who I am, where I came from and of those within my family who came before me. I am proud to be able to proclaim my heritage is Polish! This is why I searched. This is why anyone would search. To any adoption agency employee, state adoption registry employee, or more importantly, birth parent who may read this book...allow adult adoptees to have the thrill I have had. Allow them access to the information they may need or want to fill in the blanks in their lives. Allow them to become whole! This is vitally important for adoptees of earlier generations. They need the information while it might still be possible for them to meet the birth parents whom, for whatever reason, had to give them up. If the birth parent or adoptee is already deceased, then the adoption records should be opened without question.

It is *our* information locked behind vault doors and we have a right to it!

Chapter Seventeen

RETURN HOME TO BOYS TOWN

I would not return to Boys Town until 1987, nineteen years after I graduated.

It took me that long to fully realize all that it had done for me during the years I was there. Boys Town had been "my home." It was the only home I have ever known or will ever know in my lifetime.

The Boys Town Alumni Association holds a reunion every two years on the last weekend of July on the Boys Town campus. It is a time for former boys to come "home" to renew acquaintances and friendships and walk the paths they walked as young men.

For years, I had avoided these gatherings, mainly because it took me several years to realize Boys Town had been more than just a place that the foster care system had dumped me into. It had raised me, given me an education, nurtured me, given me a spiritual basis for my life and so much more. It had in fact been a "home." It was time for me to go "home" again.

Boy was "home" ever different from how I had remembered it.

Boys Town is now called "Girls and Boys Town." In 1973 the first girls were accepted onto the campus...yeah, right, wait until after I graduate! It will always be Boys Town to me.

The dormitory style living is no longer, nor are the separate living arrangements for grade and high school students. Today there are "house parents" rather than "counselors" in each living quarter. They have a family style living arrangement, with no more than eight children to a home and two to a bedroom. They eat their meals in the home rather than gathering in a huge dining room, as I had done.

Today the home accepts far fewer "homeless" children such as I was in 1961. Now, many are temporary wards of the court at the home to work out temporary behavioral problems, mandated by a court or unstable family situations. The student body has decreased from over 900 when I was there to just over 400.

No longer do many stay at the home for periods of seven years or more as I and so many of boys in my time did...the average stay today is under two years. In a sense, Boys Town today is not the community it was in the 1960s. All of us boys knew each other...we were "one family." Today it is many families in their separate homes not even attempting to be a community.

I did see some former teachers, counselors, and classmates on this trip, but I was disappointed enough that I only stayed for one day of the reunion in 1987. Though it had been "home," it had lost the feeling of home.

It would be yet another ten years before I again went "home" for a reunion. I had more feelings of it being "home" this time, and I stayed throughout the reunion weekend.

This was the first time that an alumni choir was formed to sing during mass to close the weekend. I participated and it brought back oh so many memories. Memories of Fr. Schmidt or Moe directing us, the concert tours each year and the friendships I had with so many. We rehearsed each of the three days of the weekend just as we used to every night after dinner. We not only prepared for the mass but also a short concert to be given after mass in memory of Fr. Schmidt and Moe who had each passed away in the last few years. Though the "home" itself didn't feel like "home" due to all the changes that had transpired, it was good to be back.

I returned once again in 1998. Fr. Val Peter, current Director of Boys Town, had asked if the Alumni Choir would sing the Memorial Mass to commemorate the 50th anniversary of the death of Fr. Flanagan on May 15. Fifteen of us gathered to sing the mass...all were living in Omaha except Joe from Kansas City and me from Fargo. We made sure we also had a chance to remember and eat while we were there.

The "home" continues to change. Today the students live by a whole set of rules and earn points for good or lose points for bad behavior. Privileges are based on points earned. Many of those that come do not make it through the program, as it is now called. They are sent back home or back to foster care. There appears to be more staff than students.

In my day, no matter what one might do, Boys Town worked with you to make it through to graduation. There was no such thing as failure unless you decided to go AWOL and not return. That doesn't appear to be what is happening today. Those in charge today believe that Fr. Flanagan and Msgr. Wegner did not know what they were doing in running a home for boys, despite 50 years and thousands of young men graduating and going on and making something of themselves. "I believe unless it is broken, why fix it."

Boys Town was not broken in 1973 when all the changes began happening…it may/may not be broken today…others will have to judge that. If I were at Boys Town today I would probably be among those that the current staff would have considered failures and I would have been returned to yet another cycle of moves within the foster care system. Today I could possibly be in prison or dead.

I returned to Boys Town August 29-30, 2002, with some turmoil in my life. I needed a place where, despite all the changes, I felt comfortable. I needed that quiet time once again at the tomb of Fr. Flanagan and to visit with Renato.

I also was close to Renato's younger brother, Dennis. He was two years behind us. Dennis unfortunately passed away suddenly just before Christmas 1999. I spent hours in the Alumni building talking with some who were from the "old days." We compared notes and all realized that although Boys Town had been our "home," it was not "home" anymore.

Very few of those who graduate today join the alumni association, since they don't view Boys Town as ever having been their home. It was a place they spent a year or two and then went back to their own homes. The loyalty to the home is for us old-timers and not for the newbies. Today, they are lucky to know their next-door neighbors, yet alone many of the other students.

The "Twelve Night" celebrations no longer happen, "intramural sports" are a thing of the past...even the old grade school football field has been demolished to make way for new family homes. The "Boys Town Choir," once nationally known from our tours and records, has made the heap bin of the past as has "Christmas Eve Midnight Mass." These were some of the things that made all of us at Boys Town part of the community and "our home." It is sad to see them all go.

During this trip, I found out that the last of the "old guard" has left the home. That is, all the teachers, counselors and others from my era are now either deceased or retired. The last was Dr. Pat McGinnis, who was a guidance counselor during my day. He retired in 2001 as Superintendent of Schools. The era of 1961-1968 is now history.

Going "home" again will be difficult in future years as there will be no one from the past to talk to or share memories with, except for fellow classmates. As the years go by, those will become fewer. In time, Boys Town's first 50 years will be only found in the history book of the home.

I can see now why it is even more difficult for those who were here before my time to come home...as their era has long been history. It's like going home and not finding your parents there, since they have passed. So too is that feeling, when those of us at Boys Town prior to 1968 go home. It will be "home" but at the same time it won't be...how sad it will be.

On my visit this time, a few of us who had visited in the Alumni Office decided to go to lunch in the visitor's cafe. We did not know the table we decided to sit at would put us in a front row seat to observe a ceremony. During lunch, six young men and two young women were accompanied by Fr. Peter into the café to participate in a "Citizenship Swearing-In Ceremony." Fr. Peter in his introduction, with a mural of Fr. Flanagan and the first five boys of Boys Town in the background, stated that thousands of previous students had taken this citizenship oath in the previous 85 years of Boys Town and they were about to become a part of this special village.

Those at my table could only look and wonder when such a ceremony had begun…I had never done this. I became a citizen of Boys Town just by arriving, just as one born in the USA becomes a citizen just by arriving by birth. There before a full café, the young people were to raise their right hands and take an oath of citizenship…making three promises, which I don't fully remember, as I had become upset by this point.

After taking the oath, each person then had to address those in attendance. They gave their name, where they were from, stated the names of their house parents and assistant, stated three things they liked about the home, three goals they hoped to achieve while at the home and finally what had been the hardest thing for them since arriving at the home.

I felt quite sorry for each young person as they went through this ritual. It became so obvious that the Boys Town I knew as a "home" was no more, but just another "treatment center" like those that can be found all over the country. One could tell by the comments the young people gave that they had been rehearsed so as to make a good impression. It appeared the ceremony was more for the staff gathered than for the young people themselves.

Later Friday, I went to the high school building. There in the lobby to the right-hand side in a trophy case were the trophies Jim and I had won so many years ago. I can still proudly proclaim that we were and are the best debate team Boys Town ever had.

However, some relics of the past have been scrapped. Fr. Schmidt, when he was director of the choir, had a wide collection of music and books, some extremely rare. When he left the home it was decided to just pack them up and ship them out, with those responsible not caring what they meant to those of us from choirs past…at least they ended up at the University of Pittsburgh.

For many years, Fr. Schmidt conducted a two-week Liturgical Music Workshop at Boys Town attracting renowned musicians and scholars from across the globe…it is no more!

Our memories of those days at least are preserved in a book of notes that Fr. Schmidt had written over his 36 years at Boys Town.

Many of "his boys" contributed to a fund to have the book recently published. Fr. Schmidt passed away in 1994.

Today's Boys Town may not appreciate those years of the past, even with their Hall of History, but "his boys" do.

Fr. Flanagan felt strongly that music played an important role in the overall development of a child. If he were to come back to Boys Town today I know he would ask, "But where's the music?"

I can't say if the Boys Town I remember was better than the home is today. Each has its pluses and minuses. All I know is that it is "home" for me, and for many boys of my generation.

It is my fervent hope that Boys Town still fulfills the desires of a home that Fr. Flanagan began in 1917. His belief of "there is no such thing as a bad boy" has already gone by the wayside.

Visitors to Boys Town will not see what I have put on these pages. They will see the Visitor's Center, Field House, Chapel, a few other public buildings and finally the Hall of History. They will think the Boys Town of today is the Boys Town of the past...but only those of us who lived there in the past will know the truth. It is sad also that the students of today will never know what they have missed out on.

Many say, "One can't go home again!" I will return to Boys Town for future class reunions. Though the changes continue, I will make the most of my time there. I will make it "my home" even if it is just for a weekend...it is still the only "home" I have ever known. "Home" was taken from me far too many times in my young life. I won't allow anyone to take "my home" from me now or ever!

Fr. Flanagan began Boys Town weeks before Christmas in 1917 in hopes of providing a "home" for the homeless and orphaned. His theory was if you provided the basics of food, clothing and shelter then provide an education, guidance, sports, music and most importantly a spiritual life...any boy could become a productive member of society. Thousands have. We serve in many capacities in our new home communities; many have served and died in service to their country, some followed Fr. Flanagan's footsteps and are priests...so many boys Fr. Flanagan would be proud to call "his sons" if he were alive.

Msgr. Wegner nurtured this theory for 25 years after Fr. Flanagan passed away, only in the end to be cast aside as a failure and a broken man by those of today's Boys Town. He should have been laid to rest at Boys Town but was not…it's almost like his stewardship of Boys Town never happened.

They have new theories, new rules and programs. They have made a simple job a complicated one. Yesterday a boy could come to Boys Town from the street and be welcomed with open arms; now they must be referred and financially supported. Some will make it through the programs of today while others will fail and be returned to where they came from.

I think of the thousands of kids lingering in the foster care system such as I came out of over 40 years ago…they will never get to the Boys Town I knew and will in many cases never find "the home" that I did. Some say it is progress, but it can't be progress when so many are left out and when failure is also an accepted result…a result Fr. Flanagan would have never accepted.

Unfortunately this is the Boys Town of today. I prefer to remember the Boys Town of yesterday…for it is in that yesterday that I can still see and be "at home"…the Hall of History and the classmates of my years there are all of the "home" I have left, but that is what I will grasp on to in the years yet to come.

May God bless Fr. Flanagan, Msgr. Wegner and so many dedicated men and women of the past that made a home possible for so many. May God also bless the children of Boys Town today, that despite all the changes, they may find success in their lives. Finally, may God bless those in charge of Boys Town today…may He open their eyes of the past and cause them to realize Boys Town was not a failure in 1973, and need not be today if they would but return to the very simple theories and beliefs that made it what it was in the first place…a place where so many found their first and only home of a lifetime!

This is Fr. Flanagan's final resting place in Dowd Memorial Chapel at Boys Town. I so often found peace here during my years at Boys Town. It is the first place I stop at whenever I now visit Boys Town. Still today, I cannot leave Fr. Flanagan's tomb without breaking down in tears of thanksgiving for the opportunities, hopes and determination Boys Town provided me for the life ahead.

Chapter Eighteen

BOYS TOWN TALES OF YESTERYEAR

A former boy of Boys Town cannot reflect on his past without telling a few of the tales of his years there. As a matter of fact, that is the best part of the Alumni Reunions.

Many of the adventures of years past will probably not be a part of the life of the young men and women at the home today. Life at Girls and Boys Town today is far too structured and the youth's movements tracked so closely that they cannot enjoy the freedom and adventures that those of us prior to the 80s had.

Although some experiences carried over from grade school, most of the experiences I'll share here are from my high school years, since those years allowed much of our freedom.

My stay at Boys Town came during the height of the Civil Rights Movement. There, this was not an issue, as boys of all ages, races and religions were accepted. The subject of race was rarely raised. It was not tolerated and we were all taught to get along. This was one of the things that impressed me the most during my stay there, and the "get along" lessons remain with me today.

Back in the early 1960s we grade school boys had a way of getting even with so-called tough guys. We would do a "short sheet" on them. Someone would keep watch while another guy or two would remake the tough guys bed. However, instead of making it as normal both sheets would be made up in half. That is, they were folded over in half. It looked, however, like a normally made bed.

When it came time for lights out, the tough guy would jump into bed and push his legs down into the bed. He, however, would end up tearing his legs through the sheets. Of course he would holler out, "Who did it?"

No one would ever admit to it. Everyone would have their heads under the covers trying to stifle their laughter. After a few times the tough guy either got the message or had to nightly check his bed before jumping into it.

Come to think of it; I remember doing this on occasion even while in high school.

Also back in the "old days" each living unit had a counselor and a commissioner. The counselor was an outside adult while the commissioner was one of the older boys. The commissioner was responsible for carrying out the discipline of the unit.

There was one form of discipline that stood out. Any former boy of Boys Town from the 1930s to early 1970s reading this will remember it.

The discipline was being part of the "floor shining gang." Now, bear in mind this was not done with a power shiner. Let me describe this floor buffer for you. It had a metal pole about four feet in length. Attached at the bottom was a 15-20 pound piece of square iron with bristles on the bottom of it.

This is what was used to shine the floors. One first went over the floor several times with just the brush touching the floor. Then you repeated the process with a cloth beneath the bristles.

Let me tell you, when one finished you could see your face in the floor. Your arms were also tired as heck.

I made this floor shining gang more than one time.

These floor shining relics have been relegated to the Hall of History as an exhibit. The kids of today don't know what great exercise they are missing!

This was also the primary discipline used in high school as well. Sit ups and push ups military style were usually the other discipline used.

A personal experience from grade school I remember is my first cigarette. Smoking was not allowed in grade school. Well, I had to show how big a guy I was.

One of the counselors in my building smoked Lucky Strike cigarettes. A friend and I decided we wanted to try them. We were twelve years old at the time. While the counselor was out of his office area we went in and swiped his pack of cigarettes he had left on the desk. We headed out to the old football stadium.

We each lit our first smoke. Boy, did we ever think we were cool. As luck would have it, another counselor drove by the stadium and saw us. He yelled out for us to stay put and he stopped and parked. He decided rather than taking us back to our building and turning us in, he would teach us a lesson.

He checked how many cigarettes were still in the pack and then divided them in two. He then lit each of us one and told us to go ahead and smoke. He repeated this until there were no more cigarettes. I had one whale of a headache and my stomach was also turning somersaults.

We both swore we would never ever smoke again. I wish I had kept that promise.

Only then did he have us get into his car and drive us back to our building. He didn't turn us in and we heard no more about the matter.

Dinner did not go down too well that night.

One of the highlights of most grade school boys was being able to spend an afternoon a week during the summer at the Boys Town Lake. Yes, the campus actually has its own lake. The lake remains today but times have changed as to how it is used.

Gregory Hall, where I resided during my grade school years, had use of the lake on Wednesday afternoon during the summer months. Row boats were available, as was archery. The greatest thing though, was being able to fish and what came afterwards.

If one decided to fish they could catch up to three fish. The lake was stocked with bullheads and catfish. When the afternoon at the lake was over, we were allowed to take our catch up to the grade school dining hall. There we turned in the fish, giving them our names of course! We could come back an hour later and our fish were cleaned and fried. Boy, was that stuff ever good!

You could always tell during the summer which building was having their lake day. That section of the dining hall was fairly empty as they would be outside eating their catch.

I have not fished in years but still clearly see those summer afternoons of my early years at Boys Town.

High school brought a whole new world of adventure.

Each high school boy was to have a job on campus. This is how we were to earn our thirty dollars a month we were given.

I had a great job my freshman and sophomore year. Msgr. Wegner had his home connected to the chapel. My job was to be up at 5:30 and to be at his home by 6:15. I was met by Mrs. Ann Fischer, his personal cook. Mrs. Fischer was the mother of the famous Fischer boys of the National Football League. It was my job to help prepare and serve breakfast for him. It was great working with Mrs. Fischer. She always saw that I had a snack to take to school when I left for class. She said a growing boy needed more than three meals a day.

It was during those two years that Msgr. Wegner and I got to be fairly close. Though the adults were not supposed to give us money, Msgr. always saw that I had a few dollars in my pocket. Once breakfast was served, he usually invited me to join him at the table. We always had interesting conversations.

It was at the start of my junior year that I was greeted by Msgr. Wegner rather than Mrs. Fischer one morning. He took me aside and put an arm around my shoulder. He informed me that Mrs. Fischer had been killed in a car accident the previous night. She had been like a mother to me for the two years I worked with her. I lost someone special and the tears came.

Msgr. Wegner personally took me to the funeral and then to her home afterwards to eat and to meet her sons. Apparently she had told them about me. They knew me as soon as I entered the door. It was a sad day for me.

Msgr. Wegner did not hire a new cook after Mrs. Fischer's death. Thus my job at his home ended and I moved on to work with the Director of Food Services.

Working for Mrs. Fischer and Cy is where I learned to cook and bake. A skill I still use today being a single person.

Msgr. Wegner's and my relationship, however, continued throughout my remaining years at Boys Town. His door was open to me whenever I wanted to visit with him, if he was in town.

During my senior year while I was still entertaining the thought of becoming a priest he arranged for me to spend a week at Mount Michael Abbey in Elkhorn, Nebraska. It was shortly after that week I decided it was more my desire to be like Msgr. Wegner than a real vocation making me think of becoming a priest. I decided not to enter the seminary. I believe Msgr. Wegner knew this would be my decision, but he allowed me to make it on my own rather than directing me in any one direction.

Besides getting a job when one entered high school, freshman were also required to attend summer school during the summer of transition between grade school and high school. It was thought that this would better prepare us for the new school term. Summer school lasted six weeks.

Since I had no real interest in school at that time I decided to go to the Boys Town Trade School rather than taking academic courses. I enrolled in the Bakery Program.

The Bakery Program provided all the bread as well as pastries served at Boys Town. Each was prepared daily. The highlight of the course came each day as the goods came fresh from the oven. Though we were not supposed to take any, hot, fresh Danish or bread seemed to find a way under our shirts as the class day ended. Those of us in the class had our friends gather around us as we left school to share in the goods. You have not tasted heaven until you let a piece of hot Danish with a little melted butter slide down your throat!

I remained in Trade School only that first summer as it was felt by others that I had the capability to do well in a collage prep course and I was so enrolled come that fall.

The Trade School is no more at Boys Town. The transition of the early 1980s did away with the school. This surprised me as it was here that many of the boys of previous generations as well as mine found and trained in what would become a lifetime career for them.

Courses, in addition to Bakery, were offered in Auto Mechanics, Sheet Metal, Barber Shop, Ceramics, Woodworking, Printing and Culinary Arts. Not all boys were meant for a college prep course back then and I doubt if this is any different today.

At least I can remember those fun afternoons that summer of 1964!

Basically in high school we were on our own from the time we rose at 6:00 a.m. until bed check at night around 10:00 p.m. We were responsible to see that we went to class, did our jobs, homework and any extra activities we were involved in. We had free roam of the campus.

I already told you previously of my going AWOL in my sophomore year.

Boys Town in the 60s was about ten miles from Omaha. Omaha ended at 72nd Street and farmland began. Boys Town was at 132nd Street.

Because families visited the home there was need for a motel of some sort close by. Thus the 10 Mile Inn came into being. It included small cabins as well as a lounge. Now one just cannot tempt teenagers with a place like this close at hand and not expect them to take advantage of it.

I can still recall vividly those nights a small group of us would head across the field towards Dodge Street and sneak across to the inn. Because some of the counselors would go there at the end of the day, we had to check out the place before we would go in. The man who owned the place really didn't care about age as long as one could put money on the bar.

I don't remember any of us ever getting drunk on these escapades. It was one or two beers and sneaking back to campus before the late-night walk around by the counselor to check beds. We never did get caught.

Boys Town is now surrounded by Omaha. The 10 Mile Inn is no more. The tales that place could tell if it were still standing!

I have to tell you about the escapade with Msgr. Schmidt. For this story I will call him just "Schmittie." One was not allowed to call him that while we were at Boys Town, but once we graduated he felt we earned the right to do so. Schmittie was the Boys Town choir director I spoke of before. Now Schmittie loved the good things of life. He loved his berets, his loud Hawaiian shirts, rich expensive cigars and his Chivas Regal.

I, as well as others, was always asking him to let us try his Chivas. We always got no for an answer.

Underneath the high school was a quarters where the priests on campus went for their meals as well as to relax. They had a private dining room as well as library area. This is also the space where most of them kept their alcohol…especially at Christmas time.

Schmittie seemed to get his share of bottles of Chivas at Christmas. A friend and I were determined that the Christmas of our junior year he would have one less bottle. A few days before Christmas my friend stood watch as I crept and snatched a bottle while Schmittie and a few other priests were having dinner.

We ran back to our cottage and down to the basement. I had never tasted hard alcohol before and did this stuff ever taste strong and have a bite. We had about three shots a piece and were feeling pretty good. We hid the remainder.

As we came upstairs who was standing by the doorway but Schmittie. He said he knew it had to be us who took his Chivas. Of course we denied it. He said he wanted to give us something to enjoy it with and handed us both one of his rich tasting, expensive cigars. He also reminded us that choir rehearsal was in an hour and left.

Well, I just had to have another shot of Chivas and a taste of this cigar. Back downstairs I went. My friend didn't join me.

I had two more shots and lit up the cigar. Was that ever a mistake. I don't know which caused most of the room spinning, but did it ever spin. Soon I was looking for a bucket.

Anyone in the choir did not miss a choir rehearsal. After attempting to clean up, away I went, despite the room still spinning and feeling sick.

Schmittie saw me as I entered the rehearsal hall. He just knew I was sick. All he said was, "Larry, feeling OK?" He was smiling all the while as I looked and felt like hell.

It seemed that night that he worked the baritones and basses extra hard. All the while I just couldn't wait for rehearsal to be over.

Schmittie never said another word about the incident until 1987 when I went back for my first reunion. His first words to me were, "Larry, feeling OK?" We both had a good laugh and I finally admitted his Chivas tasted pretty good and it was his awful cigar that made me sick.

It was at this reunion the alumni made a special presentation to Schmittie. He had left Boys Town about ten years earlier. The presentation was a large oil painting. Around the outer corners were various pictures of the choir. In the center was a smiling Schmittie wearing a beret, a Hawaiian shirt and a cigar in his mouth.

Schmittie has been gone since 1994 but that picture is how I remember him.

He, along with Msgr. Wegner, was the father figure in my life growing up at Boys Town. One couldn't have asked for two better ones than them!

I could go on with several more stories...but then I might think it's another gathering of alumni. We go on for hours constantly saying, "Remember when?"

As you can see, we boys of Boys Town were your typical teenage boys. One thing to the best of my knowledge that we did not partake of was drugs. This is not true of Boys Town today.

This at least gives you a taste of the tales of yesteryear. Though I didn't realize it until years later...these were very good years.

Chapter Nineteen

MEMORIES OF A LIFETIME

During the course of writing for this book I found myself in a very reflective mood. Those reflections continue as this section of the book is drawing to a close…thus this chapter.

What an unforgettable journey it has been and oh, what memories! I thought of the things I have lived through as far as history is concerned, as well as my personal experiences. There have been high and low points in both.

I recall John Glenn's memorable journey into space in 1962…a short three-orbit flight, but oh, what a flight! At age 77, he gave us all hope as we grow older, by going up once again in the space shuttle.

The hope and joy the nation had with the election of a new president in 1960 was to be shattered with the assassination of John F. Kennedy in 1963. I was in seventh grade science class when the news came over the loudspeaker that President Kennedy had been shot. Those of us in the class sat in stunned silence. Not long afterward, we heard the words, "President Kennedy is dead."

Class was dismissed, but rather than returning to the dormitories or cottages at Boys Town, there was a steady stream of boys making their way to the chapel to pray.

Throughout the three days that followed, small black-and-white televisions continually aired the various events from Washington, DC. Also, special masses were held each day in the chapel, which was full to overflowing for each one.

It was a very somber Thanksgiving Day at Boys Town, as it was just three days after President Kennedy was buried. I have been able to go to Arlington National Cemetery and visit his quite simple grave.

Would the country have taken a different course if he had survived? Unfortunately, this is a question that will go unanswered.

A brief five years later, Dr. Martin Luther King and Senator Robert Kennedy were assassinated. I had met Senator Kennedy just a few weeks earlier at Boys Town, as he campaigned for the Democratic presidential nomination. Now he, like his brother, was gone. It seemed the nation had gone crazy.

The Civil Rights movement of the mid-sixties continues in many ways, since racism and discrimination still exist today in many forms.

The Vietnam conflict, which divided our nation and cost us over 56,000 young lives, including some of my friends and classmates, also drove a president not to seek re-election. After all these years since the war ended, we still await full accounting of those brave men and women that have not come home!

America's race to the moon I still remember vividly. I was glued to the television set on that hot, sticky Sunday night in July 1969 as the lunar lander touched down and Neal Armstrong took his historic first step… "A small step for man…a giant step for mankind." That night, I felt that as a nation, we could do anything!

Watergate; what a disgrace Richard Nixon had brought to the presidency by his actions and his thankful resignation.

Who can forget the Bicentennial Celebration of 1976? I was among the millions on the shores of the New York harbor as the tall ships sailed into port, followed by the gigantic fireworks display that night. It made one proud again to be an American.

There was the disaster of the *Challenger* space shuttle exploding shortly after liftoff with the first "teacher" aboard, and the slaughter in Waco, Texas, by a madman in the name of God, watched on television across the country.

Then there was the horrific bombing of the Murrah Federal Building in Oklahoma City by one of our own that took the lives of 168 men, women and yes, even children.

I think these events brought us closer together in a small way as a nation...but soon we forgot.

We, as a nation, were stopped in our tracks the in past few years by hate crimes. James Byrd was murdered in Jasper, Texas, because he was black. Matthew Shepard murdered in Laramie, Wyoming, because he was gay. Who will ever forget the tragedy of Columbine High School? We have even seen children attacked due to hatred at a Jewish Community Center in Los Angeles, as well as Christians shot while in church in Texas. Of course, we continue to see the Israelis and Palestinians butchering each other in the name of peace and security.

September 11, 2001, we saw the greatest attack of hate upon our country when, in the name of a God, men turned planes into bombs as they crashed into the World Trade Center and the Pentagon. On that day, we also saw our first victory over this evil, as brave souls gave their lives by crashing the last hijacked plane into the quiet countryside of Pennsylvania to save others the hijackers had been aiming at...with the simple words: "Let's roll!"

When will we ever learn hate solves nothing...but it creates a never ending circle of hate?

I have lived through the presidencies of Truman, Eisenhower, Kennedy, Johnson, Nixon, Ford, Carter, Reagan, Bush, Sr., Clinton and now George W. Bush.

The discovery of the Internet...we are only just beginning to realize its potential. It will change the way our children and grandchildren live in ways we can now only imagine.

Yes, I still remember a simpler day...those early years of life when one had but a radio for music or news from the outside world. Now many of us have rooms full of electronic equipment. To me the best way still to enjoy the World Series is on radio and let the imagination run wild picturing the actual game in your mind.

History has taken may turns in my lifetime. Great achievements were accomplished, while at the same time, our nation saw eras of strife and great national grief. We have in some cases learned from our experiences, while in others, we have not and seemed destined to repeat some of our mistakes unless we make changes as a society.

Just as in our nation's history, so too has my personal life seen the same roller coaster of highs and lows.

I started life as a bastard child. I was the son of an unwed mother of 19 and a father who wanted no part of her or me. She decided long before she would give me up for adoption, and though I was never adopted, it was the best decision she ever made. I searched for, discovered and was rejected by her yet again...but it's an experience I would go through again, as it made me whole and I am the better for it.

I went to Boys Town, Nebraska, which I still call home today. I got my college degree and have been able to lead a productive life, as well as hopefully helping a few others along the way.

I discovered my roots, my real heritage, not the heritage of others. I know now that I am Polish and German and very proud of it. I have discovered, though too late to have met many of them, my great grandparents, aunt, uncles and cousins. Today I can no longer say I do not have a family or I belong to no one. I've, however, met Dorothy, Steve, Florence, David, Ann, Roger, Jerry and Carol. I have thus far also been able to write to Jon, Bill and Sue. I have been truly blessed and my heart is full.

I discovered at a young age that I was gay. I struggled for years with it and attempted suicide. Then I met a partner with whom I was blessed to share my life for 22 years. He taught me how to love and accept love, which I had never experienced before. He taught me to live my life to the fullest of my potential. Though we are no longer together today, I will always cherish those 22 years I spent with him as my partner.

The tragedy of AIDS struck my life in 1980 and remains a part of my life today. One hundred forty-one of my friends from over the years have died, including twenty-two of my closest. I still remember and think of every one of them every day.

I have lived through the verbal abuse and physical assaults only because I am gay. I felt the horror, anguish and pain at the murder of a young gay man named Matthew Shepard and realized it could have been me. It made me only more determined to fight to end hate and discrimination…not only against gays/lesbians, but for all, no matter who they are.

Yes, life, despite its ups and downs, has been good to me. I have been blessed with much. I have had a circle of close friends over the years, good health overall, despite three heart attacks, a good home and fairly comfortable life. Knowing how my life began, I can't help but be thankful each night to God for all of it.

Through the downs, I believe I have grown. They have made me a stronger and also, I hope a more caring person towards others. I have, I know, made my share of mistakes along the way. I think I have learned from them; after all, that is what life is all about. Learning, growing and maybe giving a little something back and making this world, in our own small way, a better place for our having been here.

I don't know if I am at the sunrise or sunset of my life. Whatever it is, I plan to continue living it to the fullest until the last breath is taken. We are only here for a short period of time. I plan on making the best of it with every day I am blessed to live. I think I'll be the optimist and say I am just at the sunrise of my life. I have so much I still want to do and experience.

Yes, as I look outside, I see a star-filled sky above me and reflect upon our nation's history as well as my own. I can't tell what the future holds, but I do know I will eagerly await the sunrise of yet another day.

I cannot say the wounds or pain of my life have been healed, as they have not. Those memories will remain within my heart and soul until my last breath is taken, but I will not allow those memories to control my future.

May the future offer me opportunity to be a channel of hope, warmth, comfort and love in someone else's life!

May someone say when I am gone…whenever that might be…the world is just a tad better because I was here!

Chapter Twenty

FRIENDS LOST TO AIDS ALWAYS MISSED & REMEMBERED!

This chapter is dedicated to the 22 of my closest friends lost to AIDS, from a Circle of 23. It is also dedicated to the other 118 who also lost their courageous battle against AIDS.

I cannot tell the complete story about myself without including this remembrance, as each of these men and women have played a role in my life and in some instances helped shape the man I am today.

In the summer of 1980, I stood with my partner in New York City's Central Park attending a Memorial Service for those who had died in NYC from AIDS complications. We had just lost our first close friend. The numbers from across the country were not yet 2000.

In the years that have followed, I have attended or spoken at far too many of such memorial services. I have stood by the bedside of too many friends, kissing them a final farewell, holding their hands, or giving a last hug as they have taken their last breaths. Some deaths have been peaceful while others have been agonizing...the results the same...I lost a FRIEND!

Though they have gone, some for many years now, I have not, nor will not, ever forget them. Each of them, in a special way, was a part of my life.

I continue to fight, along with so many others, to find a cure for AIDS and to see that those living with AIDS get the treatment, love and respect they so richly deserve…no matter how they got it! I hope that someday soon, we can put this dreaded illness behind us. Until then, we must *all* fight the fight. Too many, not just our community, have lost the fight to AIDS, too many in the prime of their lives. We cannot afford to lose or give up our fight.

This chapter is a time for me to remember my friends in a public way. I quietly and privately remember them each day. It is also a time I want to allow you, the visitor to my book, to remember those you may have lost.

Take a few minutes to read the words and remember your friends. Remember the good times you shared, the laughter, the sorrows and yes, the very reasons they were called your friends, family member or in many cases, life partner. Don't ever forget them and don't let others forget them either. They were real people and should not be remembered as a statistic compiled by the government.

To all of my friends, especially the Circle of 23, including Mark, the first of so many close friends to fight the fight and to meet death, looking from wherever they may be…you are missed, remembered and will *never* be forgotten!

The Circle of 23 began forming in 1972 as a group of close friends that would go to dinner, theater, concerts, Fire Island and various outdoor trips. Death from AIDS complications began overtaking our group in 1980 and twenty-three years later there was but one…me. I am the sole survivor and have not contracted HIV.

I miss my friends greatly. I think of all the times we spent together and it brings tears of joy as well as those of sadness. Each was truly a friend and a part of my life. I was very blessed with such a group!

I was privileged to be with each of the 22, except Gavin, during the final moments of life. Each a memory I will never forget. I gave the eulogy at each of their Celebrations of Life. Gavin, after struggling for almost 14 years, took his own life on June 13, 1996.

I have lost, in the many years of this battle, a total of 141 friends, each of whom was a son, daughter, husband, father, wife, mother, brother, sister or life partner of someone.

Each touched the lives of many during their all-too-brief lifetimes...each should be *remembered*, not *forgotten*! They were not a government statistic, but very real people, and with this chapter, I remember each.

I have purposely chosen not to reveal the last names, to allow them to rest and their families to have peace. There are still hate mongers in the world...if any hate is to be expressed I'd rather it is at me and not those lost or their loved ones.

I began this chapter on February 10, 1998. I have had to let it sit many times, as the pain was too much to bear at one time. Many tears of joy and sadness have been shed during its creation. May it, in a small way, allow you to remember and never forget those you may have lost.

PRAYER OF REMEMBRANCE

Today I remember my friends. Gone from my life, but not forgotten. I remember each for the love, friendship, joy and yes, even sadness, they brought into my life. I am a better person for each having been a part of my life...even but for a brief time. I ask that You wrap Your arms of love and mercy around each, as they have returned home to You. Some died without family or friends at their sides, but I am glad none died alone...for You were at their side. Give them the peace and rest they have earned. Each in their own way fought a valiant fight against AIDS, but at last they are home with You. Let them know, though they are gone from our midst...they are *remembered*, not *forgotten*. May You grant them the peace and love they so richly deserve, some not receiving either in their lifetime. May You grant them each eternal rest. Amen.

WALL OF REMEMBRANCE

1980
Mark, *Dana *Kenneth, Robert, Terry, Malcolm

1981:
Gary,*Cedric, Ryan, Bart

1982:
Larry P, Carol, Austin, Neal, Walter, John M, Renato, Susan, Donald

1983:
Jimmy, *Reginald, Louis, Gary S, Jeremy, Nick, *Michael, *Jeffrey, * Bob

1984:
Steve, *Keith, Andrew, Valerie, Dan, Roland, Mark W, Nathan, Jeff D, Winston, Steve N, James, Conrad

1985:
Austin M, *Xavier, Pedro, Vincent, Matthew

1986:
Mark T, *Audrey, Cecil, Christopher, Rob, Adam J, Edward, Thomas, Katherine, Marvin, Angie, Darrell, Dennis, Boyd, Van, Samuel, Gregory, Scott, Aaron

1987:
Nicholas, Carlton, Mark P, Kerry, Jeannie, Violet, Lawrence T

1988:
Norman, *Juan, *Jim A, *Ted, * Peter, *Joe, David W, Bradley Francis, Hank, Thomas P, Luke, Allan, Chad K, George

1989:
Anthony, *William C, Clarence, Doug, Millie, Jessica, Jim V, Steven P, Dana J, Ted, Charles

1990:
Michael K, *Patrick, *Ken D, Carl, Julius, Donald H, Stan

1991:
Mark S, *Bryce, Jacob, Curtis

1992:
Marie, Richard, Corey, Jimmy C, Nathan, Wesley

1993:
Harold, *Derrick, Joseph M

1994:
Ashley, Bob F, Vincent P, Gary A

1995:
Mike G, Tony, Ernie

1996
Gavin, *Marshall

1997:
Steve J

1998:
John R

1999:
Zack D, Timothy A, Austin P

2000:
William M, Kevin U

2001:
Jack R

2002:
Brent K

* denotes Circle of 23

Twenty-seven of those listed here answered the call and put on the uniform of their nation.

Some fought in Vietnam, Panama and Desert Storm.

Five were buried without military honors due to dishonorable discharges because they were gay. They were trained to kill another man, but could not be allowed to love one! I proudly recognize and honor their service to this nation!

This chapter is in memory of 141 friends listed above. May they each fly on wings of angels. Rest, my friends, you have earned it.

Here are a couple of newspaper excerpts of articles from my past involvement in various AIDS programs. I still participate in some, but reduced the amount of time spent back in 1998. After 18 years, I was totally burned out physically, as well as emotionally, and could not go on any further without taking time to heal.

From *The Oakland Tribune*, December 6,1990:

> The quilt is home. The Names Project's huge patchwork memorial to those who have died

from AIDS is back in San Francisco's Moscone Center.

Streams of people poured into the convention hall Tuesday night to see the quilt that has grown fourfold since it was displayed here a year ago.

Emotional scenes were repeated all over the cavernous hall.

Larry Adams brought a handful of white carnations to place on several panels he had made for lost friends, including a close friend, Norman Luers, who recently died of AIDS. The two had visited the quilt during its Washington, DC debut last year. Together, they designed Norman's panel, which includes a rainbow, pictures of teddy bears and a message that reads, "Still My Teddy Bear." "Everything on there is everything he wanted," a grief-stricken Adams said.

Organizers estimate over 100,000 people will visit the quilt during the four-day showing. The quilt includes 7,296 panels remembering a lost person to AIDS, weighing 14 tons.

Tuesday night's preview showing was slated as a reception of thanks for 1,500 people who volunteer in AIDS service programs around the Bay Area. "You are the heart, soul and the muscle," Cleve Jones, Executive Director Names Project, told the group of volunteers. "We dedicate this display to those we have lost...and we dedicate this to you."

The sea of volunteers, many who have themselves made panels for the quilt, clutched handkerchiefs and cried quietly and openly around the 2½ miles of fabric that outlined the panels.

Adams, after being consoled, said, "We're losing a whole generation of talented young people, and all that's left is a name. It's awful…it has to end."

The following was from *The Salt Lake Tribune* dated August 8, 1993:

"To Nature To Escape Isolation of AIDS!"

Coalville—AIDS has forced Jean to lead a double life. When the Salt Lake County woman first discovered she had AIDS…a few months before her husband died of the disease in 1988…she gave speeches warning others about the virus.

Her activism led to harassment and ostracism and forced her and her two daughters to go "underground."

"For every person with AIDS, there is a father, mother, brother, sister, spouse, partner or child also affected," said Larry Adams, a former Salt Lake man who has watched several friends die over the years. Recognizing that, organizers of this weekend's Camp Pinecliff retreat invited not only people with AIDS, but also families, friends and care givers.

Jean and Larry were among the 47 people who attended the camp some 18 miles southeast of Coalville.

Four years ago a similar camp was held but only for those with AIDS and a few nurses. "That was a mistake," Mr. Adams said Saturday. "What was done this time is open it up to non-infected people."

"With others invited, campers with HIV don't feel stigmatized or isolated," said Mr. Adams, who helped organize the retreat.

The activity schedule looked like any other camp agenda: hikes, volleyball, basketball and baseball. But there also were workshops on massage and stress management.

Adams said, "The community support made the retreat possible: Horizon House, People with AIDS Coalition and the MCC Church AIDS Ministry. Donations from area businesses and organizations, including $2,000 from the Salt Lake City mayor's office, paid not only for this year's camp but will make next year's retreat also possible."

Support for the camp is encouraging, but Mr. Adams stated that the AIDS crisis is over 12 years old and many still do not treat people with AIDS, their partners and their families with sensitivity. In the years that Mr. Adams has been involved in the AIDS movement, due to the deaths of several close friends, others assumed Mr. Adams also had AIDS (he does not) and ostracized him. "The gay community showed little more sensitivity than straight people did," he said.

Mr. Adams and Jean both watched long-time friends stop visiting or even calling. Jean talks tearfully of feeling isolated in her home, pretending to be simply a Mormon homemaker. For one weekend though, due to the work of Mr. Adams and others, she and others can be themselves and not have to live a lie.

Chapter Twnety-one

A FEW LESSONS FROM LIFE

I firmly believe one cannot go through life without learning a lesson or two. Though I hope I have learned my fair share, I would like to share three that I carry with me throughout each day of life.

When I have doubts about overcoming any obstacle placed in my path I turn to them. They are my source of strength.

The FIRST lesson is: Establish, maintain and cherish friends!

Look at *orchids* and *friendship*: what do they have in common?

Let's start with the *orchid*. Orchids are one of the most beautiful flowers on earth. They are fragrant and fragile yet objects of beauty. Orchids need special care when watering, feeding or adding grow lights. They need special nurturing. It sometimes can take years for a bloom to develop and open to its full beauty. The steps you take can either allow the plant to grow to full beauty or die a quick death....the final results depend strictly on *you*!

Friendship: one of the most prized assets a person can posses. It is fragile yet a thing of beauty. It requires special nurturing. It can sometimes take years to bloom and fully develop to its full beauty. The steps we take can allow it to grow to its fullest potential or to quickly wither and die...the final results depend strictly on *you*!

Have you recognized the similarities between *orchids* and *friendship*? Each are fragile yet full of beauty when we take the steps needed to allow them to develop and bloom into all their glory. Each requires our time, attention and care. Just as the *orchid* requires watering, food and even special grow lights, so too does *friendship* require them. We cannot take for granted that just because we planted the seed in either case that they will then develop and bloom on their own…if we think they can, we are in for a rude awakening when we see they have withered and died.

Whereas *orchids* need water and food, *friendships* need *you*! We need to take the time to let our friends know that we care. We need to be willing to share their bad times with them as well as the good. You can never know how a quick smile, phone call or e-mail could make the difference for them to having a good day or a bad day. Friendships should never be taken for granted as one never knows when that friend may be taken from us. Just as an *orchid* can be priceless to the gardener who cultivated them so to are *friendships priceless*. Money can buy all kinds of things in this world…but I have never known it to be able to bring a "true" friend into one's life!

Do *you* have a friend that you have neglected lately? Are some of your *friendships* being allowed to wither on the vine and die? Today would be a good day to change course…to water, feed and nurture those *friendships*. Take a moment to drop a letter or e-mail if they live distant from you. Better yet, pick up the phone and tell them you called "just because you care." Let them know you care about what is happening to them, you are there for them in their time of need and that you consider their *friendship* with you priceless and your most valuable asset. Watch the *friendship* begin to develop and bloom anew once again!

I have been blessed over the years with many true friends. They have seen me through many difficult times as well as enjoyed many good times together. Many of my friends have now passed away due to the AIDS crisis. I miss each of them greatly and they will never be forgotten as they will always be a part of my life.

Fortunately I have developed a new small circle of friends in recent years and I thank God for each of them. I hope I have been a friend to them as much as they have been a friend to me. In my five years on the Internet I have also developed a circle of friends. A few I have personally met while most I will probably never meet…their *friendship* is of no less value to me. I count them each amongst my "true" and "priceless" friends.

The SECOND lesson is: Make yourself a "gift" to others.

When we think of gift giving we usually think of birthdays or Christmas. We may look and shop for days trying to determine what the best gift is that our money can buy.

However, there is a gift we can give that would cost us no money but would be priceless to the one receiving it...it is the gift of *self.*

We need not limit ourselves to presenting *ourselves* as gifts to just birthdays or Christmas but can present *our* gift 365 days a year and make ourselves truly *gifts* for *all seasons*!

Here are 10 ways you can give of yourself to those you love, family, friends, neighbors, coworkers or the stranger in need. Think of these the next time you think you need to buy a gift.

If everybody gave this way...what a wonderful world this would be.

1. Your Time:

How many of us are too busy with our own lives to give of our time to others? Being busy is an excuse and a reason not to go out of your way. People need you and love you. They want to see you. Let them in. Let them have time with you.

2. Your Support:

How many of us really support the people in our lives? What I mean by support is encouragement and reasons to try something new, not 10 different reasons why it won't work. Just because it didn't work for you, doesn't mean it won't work for them. And, just because it didn't work for them in the past, doesn't mean that it won't work this time. There's nothing better than telling a person that they can do whatever they want in this world.

3. Your Acceptance:

This may be a toughie for some of us. This means unconditional love and the ability to love someone for who they are and not what you want them to be. It means giving up how you think their life should go, and accepting them for what they want to do with their lives. This is the greatest gift that you can give to the people in your life

4. Your Attention:

How many of us really listen to the people in our lives? For everyone who just said, "Of course I do," then why are the people in your life asking you to repeat what they just said? It's because they know that you didn't hear them. Take a few minutes, stop what you are doing, and focus on the people whom you love. Aren't they worth it? And who knows, you may even learn something that you thought you already knew.

5. Your Forgiveness:

Forgiving people for past mistakes and hurts is one of the greatest gifts you can give them. After all, they are only human. Plus, I'm sure that you haven't been the perfect human being either. Keeping hurt and anger in your life is just an excuse not to get close to people for fear that they will hurt you again. Recently I had to learn this particular step to the fullest meaning of the word!

6. Your Patience:

How many of us can't even be with the people we love because they are taking too long to tell a story or are taking longer than "you think" to complete a project that you think should take less time to get done. How do you know that there isn't a better way to do something if the people around you always have to do it your way? Having patience with people shows them that they are respected and loved. Isn't this a great gift to give?

7. Your Love:

People want to know that they are special in your life and that you care about them. If there are things that are keeping you from loving them such as conversations that you want to have with them, but you're afraid, my advice is to say it. Sometimes you have to take a risk to achieve an open and rewarding relationship. Take the risk and give your love.

8. Your Ideas:

Sometimes people want to move forward in their lives but they don't know how. You may know something that they never thought of. And who knows, your ideas may change somebody's life. So go ahead, don't be afraid to share what you know.

9. Your Smile:

There is nothing better that entering a room and seeing someone smile when you walk in. Right then and there you know that your presence makes a difference in their life. A smile is easy. You just grin upward. Plus, you burn many more calories than from frowning.

10. A Hug:

Human touch warms the heart and keeps us connected. In addition, it doesn't take much effort, it costs nothing, and it makes someone's day. Couldn't you find time in your schedule to hug someone you love today?

The greatest gift *you* can give in *all* seasons to another is...*you*!
Be the twinkle in someone's eyes...present *yourself* as the gift!

The THIRD and final lesson: Hold on to all that is within you!

Hold on to your FAITH: It is the source of believing that all things are possible. It is the fiber and strength of a confident soul.

Hold on to your HOPE: It banishes doubt and enables attitudes to be positive and cheerful.

Hold on to your TRUST: It is at the core of fruitful relationships that are secure and content.

Hold on to your LOVE: It is life's greatest gift of all, for it shares, cares, and gives meaning to life.

Hold on to your FAMILY and FRIENDS: They are the most important people in your life, and they make the world a better place. They are your roots and the beginnings that you grew from; they are the vine that has grown through time to nourish you, help you on your way, and always remain close by.

Hold on to all that YOU ARE: And all that you have learned, for these things are what make you unique. Don't ignore what you feel and what you believe is right and important. Your heart has a way of speaking louder than your mind.

Hold on to your DREAMS: Achieve them diligently and honestly. Never take the easy way or surrender to deceit. Remember others on your way and take time to care for their needs. Enjoy the beauty around you.

Have the courage to see things differently and clearly. Make the world a better place one day at a time, and don't let go of the important things that give meaning to your life.

Hold on...to each of the above...do not let them fall to the ground to be trampled by others...for they are *yours*!

No matter how many times one feels they have learned *all* the above...one can be amazed how often we need to relearn them.

I am still learning!

Chapter Twenty-two

EPILOGUE: LOST SON?

This is the question that began this book. To find the answer to it, one had to take the journey through early childhood, Boys Town, college and acceptance, search and discovery, Polish heritage and finally remembering many who played a role in my life. However, through it all light has been shed upon the answer to this question. I have thought long and hard throughout the writing of this book as well as many times prior to it as to how I might answer this question. First, I can answer that I am *not* a lost son.

Am I the son of my birth mother? No, that right was relinquished upon my birth and when given the opportunity at a second chance, she relinquished it yet another time.

I am definitely not a son of the "foster care system," for in my mind this system miserably failed me as it has thousands upon thousands in subsequent years. They moved me from place to place for years and when I became a burden to them, decided to shuttle me off to someone else as far away as possible. The only good that came out of this broken system was the Monshors becoming a part of my life and their last move for me to Boys Town.

Boys Town played an integral role in my adolescent years. It provided stability where there had been none. It provided the basic necessities of life during those crucial developing years. Yes, some there even took me under their wings as a besieged youth to let me know for the first time that I, as a matter of fact, did have potential.

Ultimately though it was also time for me to say good-bye…no, I am not the son of Boys Town.

Am I the son of my heritage? Though I am extremely happy to find my true heritage rather than having to adopt that of others, I cannot be the son of my heritage as it played no role in my life before age 36.

In the end the answer to the lost son question is an easy one. Though many played some role as to where I am today in life, I am ultimately no one's son.

If anything, I am my own son. I was responsible myself to learn the lessons of life and to make life whatever I wanted it to be.

The cards were dealt me at birth. Rather than being dealt a royal flush I was dealt maybe a pair of twos and told to play it the best I possibly could as I could not throw any cards away and hope for a better hand. I, with the help of others along the way, was ultimately responsible for how the game turned out. I could whimper and whine and just say deal me out or I could somehow attempt to make that pair of twos look like a royal flush…the choice was mine and mine alone.

I won't make the final judgment as to how well or poorly I played, others will. But, I think to this date, I have at least advanced to maybe two of a kind.

Life has dealt me many setbacks along the way to this point, but I learned at an early age to view them as opportunities and know that no matter how bad things seemed to be…they could be worse, as it is for some.

It took no special courage or strength by me to see me through these things. It took acceptance of the way things are, hard work and most importantly a deeply held inner faith in a God as I understand Him. It also took a willingness to play the cards dealt, without whining or blaming others for my position, to the best I was able. The whining or blaming would have been the easy road to take…but there are enough people on that road.

My inner faith has withstood the test of time. It has been battered and tattered but has remained intact. I have been knocked down several times through some of my own failures, but have been able to get back up and press on. It has gotten me thus far in life and I know it will see me to the end.

I said in the introduction of this book that this was a story of joy and sadness, but also of victory. The game is yet to be completed, but no matter where the winding road of life may yet take me, I believe I have already been victorious!

Fortunately for me though, I was no one's son. I had many who crossed my path and taught me the lesson that even if no one on the earth wanted me as a son I was somebody of worth; I had value and I am a good person.

Within every person there is a rose. These qualities planted in us at birth grow amid the thorns of our faults. I, in early life, had looked at myself and saw only the thorns, the defects. I despaired, thinking that nothing good can possibly come from me. I neglected to water the good within me, and eventually that good could have died. I might never realize my potential.

I did not see the rose within myself; someone else had to show it to me. One of the greatest gifts a person can possess is to be able to reach past the thorns and find the rose within another. This is the characteristic of love, to look at a person, and knowing his faults, recognize the nobility in his soul, and help him realize that he can overcome his faults. If we show him the rose, he will conquer the thorns. Then will he blossom, blooming forth thirty, sixty, a hundred-fold as it is given to him. I am thankful to have been at times surrounded with such people in my life. Without them, I don't know if victory could have been achieved.

To those who read this book and have or will face some of the same crosses and tribulations in your life as I have, please, remember, when you feel your life's crosses seem overwhelming, it helps to look around and see what other people are coping with. Many bear crosses that we can only begin to fathom. There are those with disabilities, some face terminal illness, others live poor or under dictatorships...the list is endless! You may, in the end, consider yourself far more fortunate than you imagined.

Whatever your cross, whatever your pain, there will always be sunshine after the rain.

Perhaps you may stumble, perhaps even fall, I sure have many times, but *you* have the power within *you* to stand back up, dust yourself off and overcome. *You* have it within yourself to make the most of your life no matter what the cross is you bear. Yes, I have faced many crosses in my life. I have stumbled and fallen many times despite trying to carry them. Each time, however, I have been able to pick myself up and move another step forward.

I will be honest, it has not always been easy nor has it been through my own strength...but has been combined with the strong spiritual beliefs within me. I know I will have some crosses to bear throughout my life...but I will not allow them to overburden or defeat me. I also know of the many having bigger and heavier crosses to bear than me. Mine are small and light in comparison.

If I can do it, I know each of *you* can do it! Note that people or systems along the way will fail you throughout your life. My birth parents, foster care system, found siblings and even Matt did. All one can do is accept it and get over it. But *please*...DO NOT ALLOW YOU TO FAIL YOU!

In July 2001, I suffered my third heart attack. It was very minor and was not discovered until I went to the hospital for continual chest pains and trouble breathing and the doctors noticed a new scarring on the heart. Some tests run were inconclusive, so an angiogram procedure was begun and blockage was noticed in the arteries. An angioplasty was ordered immediately. In January 2002, this procedure failed and I have since had stents placed. It took a few months to fully recover my strength and energy but I am now biking, swimming, camping and hiking once again.

In many ways today, I am still the product of my years at Boys Town. I still love music, especially classical. My soprano days of course are long gone, as now it is baritone. Singing opportunities are rare, unless you count the shower. At the Boys Town Reunion in 1997, which I attended, many of us former boys that sang in the choir gathered for our own reunion. As part of the weekend celebration we presented the Mass on Sunday followed by a concert in memory of our late directors: Fr. Schmidt and Moe.

The following year we were asked by the current Boys Town Director to come back and sing the Mass for the 50th anniversary of Father Flanagan's death…15 of us did.

I gave up playing instruments myself years ago. I had played piano, violin, clarinet and bass. Though I was not really good at any…I just loved anything musical!

One big passion I have today that I didn't have then is photography. I have albums of pictures I have taken over the years. I wish I could share some of it with you…but that might have to be another book!

In early June 2002, I decided three plus years in Phoenix were enough and I needed to return to the Midwest; the prairie never leaves you no matter where you might move! I have a new position in Dubuque, Iowa, as night operations manager for my company.

This book soon draws to a close; however it is not the end of my journey.

The search for my birth family raised far more issues than it resolved. I now want to know of the history, culture and heritage of my ancestors. I want to hopefully meet more members of my extended birth family.

Thus, one journey ended, but I am already years into this new journey. Maybe another day it will bring about yet another book.

Finally, before we part, I would recommend the chapter that follows this Epilogue. I want to share the tips I learned along the road of my journey so adult adoptees, birth families or foster children lost within the system might have a resource guide for their journey if they choose to make it. I pray it may be a useful tool to those who use it as it was to me as I traveled this road. Maybe, by providing it, your road will be prove to be easier to travel than mine, since I knew nothing about searching when I began.

I now conclude this story with a final word of advice for *all* of us: Don't live in your yesterdays, as they are done and gone. Nothing you did then can be changed. Don't live for your tomorrows, for they were never promised to you. Live for *today*...for today you have complete control over what you do, live it and live it to your fullest potential!

Peace!

Chapter Twenty-three

A SEARCHER'S GUIDE

I created this special tips chapter for adult adoptees and foster children as I am a strong proponent of "open records." I believe every person has a birth-given right to know who they are and where they and their ancestors come from.

If states will not pass open records laws for adult adoptees, they should have the right to search if they so choose. I do not believe this right should be extended to minors.

I also include foster children because of my own situation. I was placed for adoption at birth, but instead ended up in the foster care system until I aged out at eighteen. I had been totally disconnected from my birth family. Sometimes a foster child's search can be as difficult as an adoptee's.

I wish many of the tips I am including here were available to me at the time of my own search. However, despite my limitation, my search was successful.

The tips listed below are not listed by importance; only you can determine which might be important to you and what priority it is given.

TIPS:

- Create a search journal. This may assist you in keeping track of the steps you have taken in your search.

- Discuss the search with your adoptive parents. They may be willing to assist you in your search or be able to provide you with necessary information. Remember to let them know that you love them and your need to search does not, nor will not, affect your relationship with them. This will help them to not feel threatened by your need to search.
- As early in your search as possible, if you have a computer with Internet access, join adoption and genealogy newsgroups and/or support groups. They cannot only provide resources to search, but may also offer moral support during your search process.
- Locate your amended birth certificate. Write your State Office of Vital Records for it.
- Obtain a copy of your final decree of adoption. Write the court that finalized the adoption for it.
- Obtain your petition to adopt. The same court that finalized your adoption should have this as part of their records.
- Contact the adoption agency that placed you to obtain non-identifying information. You may possibly receive information you might not expect.
- Contact the law firm or attorney who assisted in your adoption for the same reason as above.
- Contact your delivery physician again for the same reason as above.
- File a waiver of confidentiality with the adoption agency, law firm and courts. This will allow your information to be released to a birth parent or sibling in the event they are searching for you.
- Apply for medical records from the hospital where you were born *only if* you have the name of your birth mother and/or father. Adoption should not be mentioned as you may find this avenue immediately closed to you.
- Attempt to retrieve your original (pre-adoption) birth certificate. You may not receive it, but you have nothing to lose by requesting it.
- Formally petition the court to open your adoption records. To forward identifying information, the court will need a reason. An example would be a medical reason. Unfortunately this has not proven very successful, but again, an avenue to try.

- Register with the International Soundex Reunion Registry (ISSR). Also, if the state in which you were adopted has an adoption registry, register with it. This allows the registry to release information if family is looking for you.
- Check both county and state records for marriage or divorce records for either birth parent. If you
- Know the names of your birth parent(s) this will be a very useful tool, especially if your birth parents were, in fact, at one time married.
- Learn about the adoption laws for your state. Ignorance of the law is not an acceptable excuse.
- Check county or state death records for birth parents and both grandparents. This record will include who provided the information on the certificate, as well as the funeral home involved. The funeral home could provide you names, addresses and possibly phone numbers of survivors. Requesting my maternal grandfather's death certificate, on a hunch that he was deceased, is what unlocked all the doors for me in the search for my birth mother.
- Send for a copy of Where to Write for Birth, Marriage, Divorce, and Death Records available from: Superintendent of Documents, US Government Printing Office, Washington, DC 20402.
- Write to Adoption Regulation Unit to access your adoption records.
- Order a copy of *The Guide to Genealogical Records* in the National Archives from: The National Archives, Washington, DC 20408.
- Find maps for the area where you are searching.
- Create a profile of the hometowns or regions where each of your birth parents is said to have been from.
- Create a list of all the libraries in your area and the areas where you are focusing your search. They will be a good source for finding obituaries for family members who may be deceased. The obituaries will list survivors, which may lead you to your birth family.
- Check local newspapers from where you were born for birth announcements. Your local library usually has old newspapers going back several years.

- Check local newspapers from the area where your birth parents were born for their birth announcements.
- Check local newspapers for wedding and engagement announcements for your birth parents.
- Check in old city/telephone directories to try to locate your birth parents or other relatives. These can be found at many local libraries or historical societies. I tracked my maternal grandfather for over thirty years using this resource. When his name suddenly disappeared, I then requested a death certificate from the state.
- Check in city directories to match an occupation to a name. Some older city directories actually listed companies where people worked. Finding out where my paternal grandfather had at one time worked led me to my birth father's sister and eventually to my birth father.
- Cross reference city directory information year by year.
- Check in city directories to locate old addresses of birth parents and possible neighbors. Former neighbors of a birth parent may be able to tell you where they might be now.
- Check current phone books and national telephone directory discs for birth relatives. Check with your phone company for availability.
- List yourself in the telephone directory of the area where you were born, and in the area where you live now. An unlisted number could lead to a dead end for someone who might be searching for you.
- Check any possible surnames against a book of name deviations.
- Speak with your local librarian. They will prove to be invaluable in directing you to many of the resources in this guide.
- Locate all churches of the faith of your birth parents in the area where they were living at the time of your birth and where they may live now.
- Check local churches in the area where you were born for any baptismal, marriage or death records.
- Check local churches in areas where you believe your birth parents may have resided for their baptismal, marriage, or death records.

- Join a local or national search and support organization, and sign their registry if they maintain one. Support of others during the very stressful search process will prove invaluable to you and they may also be able to provide tips and clues for you to use. One group that proved very helpful during my search was ALMA (Adoptee's Liberation Movement Association). Most major cities have a local chapter.
- Create your own library of search and reunion books.
- Advertise in adoption search magazines. Be sure to list your "birth name" if you know it as well as your "adoptive name."
- Advertise in newspapers where you believe your birth parents may now reside.
- Order a copy of *How to Locate Anyone Who Is or Has Been in the Military*. 1-800-937-2133.
- Contact old neighbors for forwarding addresses and other possible information.
- Visit old neighborhoods in person to locate past acquaintances of your birth parents.
- Check with former employers about possible forwarding addresses of birth parents.
- Check old high school and college yearbooks in the areas of your search.
- Check with high school or college reunion chairmen about the current address of a birth parent or request a list of entire class.
- Contact a private investigator or consultant. I suggest this only if all else leads to a dead end. Investigate any investigator before hiring them.
- Request from the court that finalized your adoption the appointment of a Court Investigator. The CI will attempt their best to locate a birth parent or sibling. However, they will only be able to provide non-identifying information directly to you. They will ask you to write a letter to the person found without identifying information. All communication will be through the CI. Only if the person found agrees to have contact made can the CI then assist in a reunion or the exchange of identifying information. A fee is charged.

- Leave no stone unturned...you never know where you might find the gold nugget of information you have been looking for!

Might I make one more suggestion? If you find your birth parents and a reunion is planned here is an idea for a gift. Make a book that might include pictures, any news articles of accomplishments and possibly a letter about you, why you searched and that you are happy you located them.

When I met my birth mother for the first time, I gave her a red rose for each of the thirty-six years of the life she had given me. As I left her suite at the end of our first day together, I gave her "my book" so that she could read it privately after I left. When I met her the next morning she greeted me with tears, a hug and a thank you. Despite how our relationship ended twelve years later, I believe that book is something she treasured for the rest of her life. She passed away in October 2001.

This guide of tips does not guarantee success. It is a tool to use in your search and not an all-inclusive one at that.

I hope you will find it useful and I further hope your journey will in the end meet your goal.